How Right Is the Right?

How Right Is the Right?

A Biblical and Balanced Approach to Politics

Randall L. Frame & Alan Tharpe

ZondervanPublishingHouse
Grand Rapids, Michigan

A Division of HarperCollinsPublishers

How Right Is the Right?
Copyright © 1996 by Randall Frame and E. Alan Tharpe

Requests for information should be addressed to:

📖 ZondervanPublishingHouse
Grand Rapids, Michigan 49530

Library of Congress Cataloging-in-Publication Data

Frame, Randall L.
How right is the right? : a biblical and balanced approach to politics /
Randall L. Frame and Alan Tharpe.
p.   cm.
ISBN: 0-310-20374-0 (pbk.)
1. Christianity and politics—United States.   2. Conservatism—Religious
aspects—Christianity—Controversial literature.   3. Evangelicalism—United
States—History—20th century.   4. Christianity and politics—Biblical
teaching.   5. United States—Politics and government—1993-   I. Tharpe,
Edgar Alan.   II. Title.
BR526.F53   1996
261.7'0973—dc20   96–17505
                                                                   CIP

Printed in the United States of America

96 97 98 99 00 01 02 03 /❖ DH/ 10 9 8 7 6 5 4 3 2 1

To Rodger, my brother, who told it like it was

RANDY FRAME

To my wife, Margaret, whose patience and endurance have demonstrated real caring. To my children—Jason, Shawn, and Jamie—who taught me patience and how to keep growing and learning and who are my real accomplishments. And to my parents, Rev. Ed and Dr. Gertrude Tharpe, and my brother, David, and my sister, Jeanne, who have provided much love and assistance

ALAN THARPE

Contents

Preface

As Alan and I worked on this book, it occurred to both of us times that our whole lives have prepared us for the task. Our experiences, it seems, have reinforced our inclination to notice life's mysteries and paradoxes more than its certainties.

For a long time I have been aware that my values, feelings, instincts, and perspectives do not fit neatly into any of the major ideological molds that others believe offer all the answers we need. I believe, for example, that the Protestant work ethic—that a good's day's work should precede a good day's pay—is at heart a biblical notion. By contrast, having spent some time as a child "on D.P.A." (Department of Public Assistance—the '60s version of welfare), I can't help but take personally the arguments for wholesale abandonment of the system.

Having grown up in a small, blue-collar-to-the-core coal town in western Pennsylvania, I experienced a heavy dose of cognitive dissonance upon my entry to the evangelical subculture. Prior to my senior year of college, I had never heard of Wheaton, IL or *Christianity Today* magazine. I would soon become intimately familiar with both. And as I did, I discovered that shared affirmations of faith did little to quell my constant unease with cultural and social values that I had trouble understanding, let alone evaluating. Who would have dreamed when I started working at *CT* in 1982 as a news reporter that I would go on to write more words for that publication than anyone else in its distinguished history?

The stories on which I reported only heightened my appreciation for life's ambiguities. Whether a church school controversy in North Platte, Nebraska, or a nuclear arms conference in Pasadena, California, I walked away shaking my head. It was easy for me to be unbiased, since I had no idea which side was right or wrong. My hesitancy was based in part on the recognition that amid the thoughtless extremists on both sides could be found intelligent, sincere, good-hearted Christians who simply disagreed.

In the mid-1980s, one of my journalism colleagues left to join an advocacy-type ministry. He explained that he had spent enough time figuring out the answers and it was now time to go apply them. I half-wondered whether I would do the same when I hit age forty. But now, even though I am still a few years away, I already know it is not going to happen with me. If anything, I expect to have even more questions. I only hope that the quality of my questions will improve.

—Randall L. Frame

Growing up in Hawaii, I became aware that I was different from most of my friends. Living in the South during the civil rights movement, I became aware that accepted answers did not match my beliefs. My seminary and graduate education reinforced my sense that we needed to wrestle with serious questions and listen to other viewpoints. As finite, sinful human beings, we cannot know everything. We might, in fact, be wrong. However, we must also act. Thus, my struggle has been to learn how to firmly believe something, act on that belief, and yet truly listen to others. Listening to others means that we have to believe that they might be right and we might be wront. For me, then, the search for what is right—the search for God's will—is a never-ending search. The Christian pilgrimage is a journey that takes a lifetime. Asking questions and listening to others and God is at the origin of all such journeys.

Thus, the purpose of this book is not to reveal conclusive and undebatable truth. Rather, it is to outline and advocate a process by which we can live together with civility amidst our many disparate, seemingly incompatible perspectives. This process, Randy and I hope, will move Christians in the direction of discovering answers together and respecting one another until we do.

—Alan Tharpe

The authors take full responsibility for this book's content, but wish to express our thanks to the following for contributions of various kinds and sizes: Fred Clark, Craig McLain, Heidi Rolland, Dave Unander, Stan LeQuire, Denise Ratcliffe, Tony Campolo, Jeron Frame, and last but not least, Chris "Go Deeper" Hall.

Introduction

Our political system is broken. H. Ross Perot has said it. Bill Bradley has said it. And millions of Americans believe it and are saying it too.

We've witnessed too many symptoms to deny that the system is broken. Too many leaders care more about winning arguments than telling the truth. Too many organizations care more about raising money than behaving with integrity. Too many politicians care more about winning elections than doing what is right for people and for the country. And too many individuals, including those who carry the banner of Christ, would rather make villains of their opponents than try to understand them. The system is definitely broken. We want to help fix it.

Much of the problem can be summarized in seven words: "Hardened ideology runs rampant in the land." Defined as a set of presuppositions and working hypotheses, an ideology ideally functions as a helpful framework that guides the search for truth. But if that framework becomes closed to new possibilities and ideas, it becomes a master instead of a servant.

By and large, commitment to political ideologies of Left and Right in our country has supplanted the reasoned debate necessary to move toward workable solutions to the problems we face. Those on the extremes gave up on honest, respectful dialogue long ago. With that, they gave up on the possibility that truth can be discovered at various points along the political spectrum.

Social polarization, based on uncompromising ideological commitment, has by no means escaped the church, including the evangelical church. Despite the Christian Coalition's claim to represent 40 million believers, those who follow Christ are divided politically. The concept of a common spiritual mission that transcends those political differences has gone into hiding. This may be the most significant casualty of what some describe as the current culture warfare.

The country's recent fascination with Colin Powell notwithstanding, to stand somewhere between—or outside—the major party ideologies may be the shortest path to political voicelessness in this era where extremists get all the attention and where the formula for political success calls for oversimplifying the issues and "demonizing" political opponents. But to take such a stand is exactly what many politically moderate evangelicals, including the authors, feel they must do.

We believe that this bloc of moderate evangelicals, the "Moral Minority" if you will, represents the best hope for repairing the broken system. We have in mind people of faith who can neither decide once and for all between political Left and Right nor feel it necessary to decide. They identify with some of the political inclinations—and support some of the public policies—both of political "liberals" and "conservatives."

The hope represented by evangelical moderates, however, is not based primarily on specific public policy positions. Rather it is represented in the attitudes, principles, and priorities they can bring to the political debate. For if inflexible commitment to ideology lies at the root of the problem, the solution is not merely to carve out a third ideology that lies between the two extremes. Instead the solution must focus on the development of a new paradigm, a new model to guide the political discussion.

This implies, as it should, that we are not satisfied with the model constructed by the so-called Christian Right. In addressing the question, "How Right is the Right?", we will attempt to give credit where it is due. But we will also argue that the approach to politics favored by many organizations of the Christian political Right has serious, negative implications for the witness and mission of the church.

In Part 1, after introducing and describing some of the frustrations of evangelical moderates, we will critique the Christian

Right, focusing on its impact on the mission of the church. Then we will examine how hardened ideology short-circuits intelligent, thorough debate.

We conclude Part 1 with chapter 5, the centerpiece of the book: "The Ten Commandments of Moderate Political Behavior." This chapter consists of ten clearly stated principles that, if applied, would go a long way toward loosening the chains of ideological captivation without compromising the moral voice the church must uphold to the world. These commandments presume that, particularly when it comes to matters of public policy, sincere, intelligent people—including Christian people—can and do disagree. They also presume that Christian citizens, without denying the differences among them, can and should make an effort to live together peacefully amid their disagreements and disparate priorities.

In Part 2 we will illustrate how our ten commandments might find application to many of the most important and divisive issues of our time, including abortion, homosexuality, and the church-state debate. Much of our analysis will focus on the Religious Right, which is enjoying unprecedented political power across the United States. In the concluding chapter, we will summarize the principles and positions advocated throughout the book in the form of a proposed "Agenda for Evangelical Moderates."

The way of political moderation in contemporary America may be a lonely life, but by no means do we feel alone. For we believe that the presence of a politically moderate, though largely unconnected, bloc of evangelicals in this nation is far more substantial and potentially influential than is commonly understood or acknowledged. We hope this book will play a role in providing a voice for this silenced segment of our society, and perhaps even serve as a rallying point for greater political organization and participation. More importantly, we hope it will contribute to the important goal of unifying Christians of all political stripes.

Above all, we hope that the lasting contribution of this book will be not its critique of the Right, but its presentation of biblically based principles to guide the political debate and to steer us through this uneasy time of perceived culture war.

Part One

Chapter One

Evangelical Moderates: Alone in America

I've been reading my Bible for fifty years and I can't
find any Party affiliation for Jesus.

Congressman Charles Stenholm of Texas at the
Christian Coalition's 1995 Road to Victory conference

The centerpiece of democracy is a small, curtained chamber called a voting booth. But for millions of Americans in recent decades, this hallmark of democracy has become a major source of frustration. On the one hand, we have been told since grade school that it is our civic duty to vote. But most feel that if we are willing to go to the trouble of voting, we might as well vote for someone who stands for principles in which we believe. Therein lies the rub. Such persons have become harder and harder to find.

Perhaps Americans are spoiled. Especially for those accustomed to having 33 flavors of ice cream and 52 television channels from which to choose—two options on Election Day simply will not do. Many acknowledge their responsibility to vote, but they also believe the system has a responsibility to produce candidates significant portions of the electorate can support with at least a modicum of sincerity and enthusiasm. This has not happened.

It comes as no surprise that only about one-third of Americans typically vote in Congressional elections. In the last Presidential election, only 39 percent bothered.[1] No doubt some people eschew polling places because they don't want to miss their favorite day-time TV game show, soap opera, or talk show. But many others simply cannot muster the energy to break up their day just for the privilege of deciding which candidate is the least undesirable. People are frustrated.

To their credit, politically conservative Christians have in recent years done something about their frustrations. Led by the 1.7 million-member Christian Coalition, organizations on the Right have gone to work politically to create the options they desire.

Many evangelicals and fundamentalists have been pleased with the fiscal conservatism—less government and lower taxes—that has unified the Republican Party since the election of Ronald Reagan in 1980. But they are disenchanted with the GOP's inclusive, "big-tent" approach to social and moral issues such as abortion and homosexual rights. The growing political power of the Christian Right has increasingly forced a Republican Party united by economic issues to choose between ignoring social and moral issues and casting its lot with the social conservatives. Spokespersons on the Christian Right, including James Dobson, maintain that the Republican tent is not big enough for both.

But if the Republican Party represents at least a potential home for some conservative Christians, for others, including political moderates, no home is in sight. In general, evangelical moderates cannot in good conscience embrace some of the Democrat Party's social liberalism, represented, for example, by its uncompromising advocacy of abortion as a constitutional right. Nor do they feel comfortable with much of the Republican Party's political and social agenda as it relates to such concerns as the environment, minority rights, and the poor. In other words, they have no place to call home.

Few politicians bridge the gap between the political ideologies represented by the GOP and the Democratic Party. The differences among major Democratic candidates for President are generally minor and usually related to secondary issues. Often they merely advocate somewhat different means to accomplish the same end.

In any case, what separates the party's Presidential candidates is not issues, but charisma and "electability."

Except for some distinctions based on social issues that the Christian Right has forced within the GOP, Republican candidates offer pretty much the same prescription for what ails the country. As Pat Buchanan said in September of 1995, when 10 Republicans were vying for the White House, "All ten would make better Presidents than the guy who's in there now."[2]

To be sure, Democrats beat up on one another during primary season, and Republicans do the same. But they try not to inflict any mortal wounds and they eventually unite to oppose the other party. Even in the most bitterly contested primary races, the candidates always seem to be able to kiss and make up in time for the fall elections.

A two-party system militates against the consideration of an issue on its own merits. All issues become part of a "package deal." To succeed, politicians must buy the whole package. Based on how a Senator or Congressman articulates his or her position on abortion, one can almost always tell where that person stands on virtually every other major political and social issue. Christian Coalition scorecards typically give members of Congress either a 100 percent or a zero percent rating, which makes it difficult for those who like—and dislike—some elements in both packages.

The anonymity and loneliness of evangelical moderates is due in part to the mainstream media, for whom the idea of a politically moderate evangelical constitutes a news flash. Most media folk assume that theologically conservative Christians are, by definition, Republicans. To be sure, many such conservatives provide justification for such a presumption, having defined their Christianity in terms of Republican political principles and ideals while treating the Democratic Party as the focus of evil in the world, or at least the country.

But surveys reveal far more political diversity among believers than is commonly acknowledged. According to a CNN/USA Today/Gallup poll in August of 1995, more self-described evangelicals voted for Clinton than for Bush in 1992. According to this same poll, 37 percent of evangelicals said they planned to vote for Democratic Congressional candidates in 1996.

An Election News Service exit poll concluded that 75 percent of evangelicals voted Republican in 1994.[3] But according to a *Time*/CNN survey in November of 1995, 36 percent of those who identify with the "Christian Right" said they favored Clinton over Presidential candidate Robert Dole.[4]

We recognize that not all surveys are equally valid. Yet unless all of these previously cited surveys are flawed, it seems clear that the conservative religious community is far from monolithic, especially when theologically conservative African-Americans are included in the mix. Certainly, the Christian Coalition's claim to represent 40 million evangelicals is open to question. Few would contest the notion that a significant number of theological conservatives—evangelicals, if you will—identify with the general political philosophy and policy goals of the Republican Party. But many evangelicals find points of light in both major parties as well as points of darkness. Their ideal political platform would consist of elements from both major party programs. If given the opportunity, they might also want to add, based on the values they derive from Scripture, some ideals and principles currently absent from both parties.

We believe that moderates have the potential to make contributions to the church and to the society disproportionate to their smaller numbers. To the church, evangelical moderates represent the hope of presenting to the world a unified witness based on moral principles, a witness that is distinct from politics and thus transcends the stifling barriers of political disagreement. To society, because they have a foothold in both ideologies, moderates represent the desire of most Americans to move the political discussion and debate beyond the current political ideologies so that issues can be considered separately and on their own merits, as they should be.

Evangelical moderates, we believe, are in the best position to model a new paradigm for political debate, a model characterized in large part by the recognition of ambiguity, uncertainty, and conflicting facts and analyses of complex social problems and issues, a model that allows tentative conclusions and working hypotheses to take precedence over premature conclusions dictated by political expediency. Because of these characteristics, however, moderates will constantly have to fight the stereotype of being lukewarm or "wishy-washy."

Related to this is a desire among some evangelicals for a kind of certainty that the Bible does not promise. For example, some people need to believe that the King James Version is God's final word for humankind, even though the KJV translators themselves favored a variety of translations. Other people have an overwhelming need to solve the mysteries of the end times, which perhaps explains the sales of millions of copies of Hal Lindsey's *Late Great Planet Earth*. Moderates, however, are simply unable to match extremists' offer of a black-and-white world, complete with a detailed description of the enemy and a clear sense of direction on all public policy issues.

This felt need for certainty carries over into the world of politics, as evidenced in part by the Christian Coalition's ordination of conservative political positions, which are allegedly based on biblical principles. In contrast, moderates are prepared to acknowledge that in the political realm, certainty is often an elusive reality. This approach may never have much market value. But we ought to dispense with the assumption that moderates are, by definition, lukewarm.

The content of moderate positions should not be confused with the fervor with which moderates hold to those positions. Many moderates are every bit as passionate and dedicated to their convictions as their extremist counterparts. But their conclusions do not land them solidly in one political camp or another. And their convictions lead them to challenge—and sometimes to abandon—the political process because of how it currently works. Among moderates' chief political conclusions is that we should all be more tentative about reaching uncompromising political conclusions. This flies in the face of the way ideologues operate, and currently ideologues are in control of the nation's political process.

This is not to say that moderates affirm nothing with certainty. As with other Christians, moderates also believe their positions are based on biblical principles. But the "rightness" of biblical values notwithstanding, moderates stress that there are proper and improper ways to bring those values to bear on the society. Among the biblical values that we uphold is the recognition of the freedom of others, including non-Christians, to disagree.

Moderates recognize that absolute biblical principles do not readily translate into absolute public policies. They realize that their perspectives and beliefs must simultaneously wield influence upon, and coexist with, competing values in the marketplace of ideas in this diverse, pluralistic democracy.

A moderate approach eschews brute political force in favor of reasoned discussion and consensus wherever possible. It advances "fair rules of fighting," not unlike the kinds of rules advocated by James Dobson and other Christian counselors intended to serve married couples when they do not see eye-to-eye. Finally, it recognizes the important place of "agreeing to disagree," which suggests a level of mutual understanding and respect that is lacking when opponents simply walk away angry.

We hope and believe that the principles for moderate political behavior presented and promoted herein will lead to increased civility and mutual respect among those of disparate political orientation. Among other things, we will urge that people with different views not treat one another as enemies, as targets for character assassination, innuendo, and stigmatization.

We appeal to those who identify with this description of evangelical moderates to model these principles, which are intended to advance a more reasoned, intelligent discussion of the issues. Over the long haul, we believe that such a discussion is in the best interests of everyone.

Chapter Two

How "Christian" Is the Coalition?

As Christians in politics, we must be as humble in spirit as we are noble in aspirations. The way we love our neighbors and the fact that we love our enemies must be hallmarks of our existence.

U.S. Senator John Ashcroft of Missouri at the
Christian Coalition's 1995 Road to Victory conference

An analysis of the Religious Right should not end with the Christian Coalition—it must begin there. The flagship organization of the Christian Right, the Coalition claims a membership of nearly two million and a following of many more millions. As reported by Pat Robertson at last year's conference, the publication *Campaigns and Elections* alleges that the Christian Coalition is "dominant" in 18 states and "substantive" in 13 more. Robertson added that he would not be satisfied until the Coalition wielded political power in all 50 states.

Christian Coalition executive director Ralph Reed has consistently contended that the organization's devotees represent mainstream American political and social values. He and others on the Right maintain that these values have been largely abandoned in recent decades by the powers that be, including the liberal political establishment, the public education system, and the media.

Politically conservative Christians believe they have been denied their rightful place at the table of political discussion. Their efforts at political organization are merely the attempts of patriotic, Bible-believing American Christians to exercise their constitutional rights and have their political voices heard. What could possibly be wrong with that?

Critics of the Christian Coalition and other organizations that make up the Christian Right have found plenty wrong with it, ranging from allegations of "stealth" campaign tactics to charges that the Right wants to create a theocracy in America. However, though we disagree with some of the Christian Coalition's political positions, what we find "wrong" with it boils down to just one thing: its name.

It should go without saying that in America people of any religious belief or of no religious belief have the right to exercise their political freedom, including the formation of political organizations of like-minded people. They have the right to educate voters and to take stands on issues, though tax-exempt organizations such as the Christian Coalition must stop short of endorsing specific candidates. So far, the Coalition has abided by this principle, or at least no one has successfully proved otherwise.

People who organize for political purposes also have the right to call themselves whatever they want, including the "Christian Coalition." We do not question the legality of this name. But in view of the more important spiritual mission of the church, we strongly question its truthfulness and its wisdom.

The name "Christian Coalition" is either disingenuous or potentially damaging for at least two reasons. First, it implies that this organization represents *the* Christian position on political issues, as opposed to representing a particular political perspective, one with which some Christians agree and others disagree. What the Christian Coalition ultimately wants is not public policy based on Christian principles, but public policy based on its own particular version of Christian principles. This version does not represent the body of Christ as a whole, even if it does speak for the majority of believers.

For the record, Reed and other spokespersons for the Coalition have acknowledged that not all Christians agree with the organization's political conclusions. But this concession to political diversity among Christians receives virtually no attention at the Coalition's conferences or in its literature. Instead, it frequently claims to speak for the country's 40 million evangelical voters.

Virtually all evangelical Christians agree with the Coalition's analysis of and perspectives on *some* political issues. But many of the issues on which the group takes a stand are matters of political judgment, not Christian principle. As we will discuss in more detail in chapter 3, to identify the mission of the church with a particular political program is to risk degrading the church's essentially spiritual mission.

Second, we oppose the name "Christian Coalition" because it implies that the organization focuses on Christian activity, as over against political activity. "Politics, for us, is a mission field," says Reed.[1] And we agree that political involvement can be seen as a Christian calling. But Christians who are involved in the political realm, as in any field of endeavor, must conduct themselves in ways that distinguish them from their non-believing counterparts, in ways that point others toward Christ. As we will soon illustrate, the Christian Coalition's modus operandi owes more to power politics than to biblical principle.

In a confusing statement at last year's Road to Victory conference, Pat Robertson said the organization was named "Christian Coalition" because he wanted it to be inclusive of others, including Jewish people. But including "Christian" in the name seems to militate against a goal of inclusivity.

We contend that the Coalition is, at heart, a political organization. Its membership is open to all people—not just Christians—based on political agreement, not on shared faith. In his book *Politically Incorrect*, Reed discusses what he calls the "new ecumenism" taking place among conservative Christians, Catholics, and the Jewish community. Thus the catalyst for the unity is politics, not faith.

To defend the claim that the Coalition's method of operation is primarily political, we must distinguish between those attitudes and actions that reflect Christian values and those that are motivated by political considerations. In the political arena as well as everywhere else, Christian conduct should be characterized by an honest pursuit of truth and by the consistent affirmation of moral principles even if this crosses the boundaries of competing political ideologies. In addition, Christian behavior is distinguished by the commitment to treat opponents fairly and with respect. This includes representing their positions responsibly and completely. As Arkansas lieutenant governor and conservative Christian Mike Huckabee puts it, "Let us be the people who win not because we bust the kneecaps of our opponents and disable them in the contest, but because we offer better ideas."[2]

In contrast, according to the rules of politics, a high premium is placed on winning, whether on the floor of Congress or on Election Day. Politics is driven by the goal of gaining power and keeping it. In accordance with that goal, truth is not affirmed in a disinterested way. Instead, facts are cited selectively based on whether they support the immediate political objective. Ethical considerations become secondary, important only if they threaten to impinge on the larger goal of political victory. Thus the "sin" of Watergate was not what anyone did, but that someone got caught.

Misrepresenting opponents' positions and treating political enemies with sarcasm and derision are morally questionable activities. Unfortunately, we have come to accept such behavior as inevitable in the political arena. Those who can't stand the heat are advised to leave the kitchen. Any urge to treat others fairly and decently must bow before the pragmatic philosophy of politics: "Whatever it takes to win."

The Christian Coalition is by no means devoid of Christian principle or moral sensitivity. But we offer the following observations of the organization's 1995 Road to Victory conference to establish that its essential character is political. (Based on our knowledge of other Coalition events and similar conferences of Christian Right organizations, we are confident that the 1995 conference fairly represents the movement.)

Well-known conservative William Bennett, a favorite at Coalition conferences, aptly illustrates the mentality characteristic of political behavior. At the Road to Victory conference, Bennett was lauded for daring Time-Warner executives to a face-to-face meeting to read the lyrics they were willing to market to America's youth. The executives refused and Bennett was hailed as hero.

But even the courage of heroes like Bennett has its limits. For example, he did not say to his Coalition audience what he said on *This Week with David Brinkley* barely a week later: "There are pro-choice [Presidential] candidates I could support." Had he stated such sentiment at the Christian Coalition conference, he would have been booed out of town. In addressing the Coalition, Bennett said only what was politically correct and expedient. This is the mentality of politics, not of prophets, for a prophet does not permit the context to influence the message.

The Coalition's historians of record also serve to illustrate the organization's essentially political character. Neither David Barton nor Peter Marshall has degrees in American history. But both are regularly held up as experts at Coalition events, including Road to Victory 1995, where both were featured prominently. Barton and Marshall maintain that God has chosen America to fulfill a unique mission in the world. According to Marshall, "America is God's project, a divine experiment in self-government." Both Marshall and Barton believe this nation was founded as a Christian nation, yet they give no serious attention to the negative chapters of America's past.

Barton's propensity to take historical and legal facts out of context is well documented by political scientist John R. Vile, who attended a rally at which Barton spoke.

Discussing the 1963 Supreme Court case of *Abingdon v. Schempp,* Barton claimed the Court said in its ruling that Bible reading could cause psychological harm.[3] Vile points out that the Court's statement in this regard was a reference to the testimony of someone commenting on the impact on a Jewish child of reading the New Testament in a public school. The Court's written opinion affirmed "the place of religion in our society as an exalted one."[4]

Strangely, Ralph Reed, who holds an earned Ph.D. in history from Emory University, makes no mention in his book *Politically Incorrect* of the contributions of Barton or Marshall. We suspect he would agree with our opinion that, as a Christian historian, neither one has the stature of Mark Noll, George Marsden, and Martin Marty. But the mixed reviews of America's past that Noll, Marsden, or Marty might offer at a Road to Victory conference would have a stifling effect on the Christian Coalition's political goals. Politics prevails; Barton and Marshall are useful.

Something important is revealed also in the way Coalition members treat fellow human beings. Speaking to the Coalition, Reed stated, "My prayer today is that, as the world looks at you and looks at us as a movement, they do not see Republicans or Democrats or conservatives or liberals, but they see followers of a humble carpenter from Galilee."[5] Given the way the world views the Coalition, it is clear this prayer has yet to be answered.

As Reed spoke, advocates of homosexual rights gathered outside. They held signs of protest across the street from the Washington Hilton Hotel. One conference attendee shouted to the protesters that he was not concerned about them since they would all be dying of AIDS anyway.[6]

Reed, we are confident, would find such a statement and the attitude behind it appalling. But the example he set in his own address at Road to Victory 1995 was far from stellar. In that address, he encouraged Coalition members to sign a pledge card addressing how they should conduct themselves. The card, he explained, was based on a similar pledge that guided the activities of Martin Luther King, Jr., and his Southern Christian Leadership Conference in the 1960s. He cited the following admonitions on the card:

1. Meditate daily on the teachings and life of Jesus.
2. Remember always that the movement seeks justice and reconciliation—not victory.
3. Walk and talk in the manner of love, for God is love.
4. Pray daily to be used by God so that all men might be free.

5. Observe with both friend and foe the ordinary rules of courtesy.
6. Seek to perform regular service for others and for the world.
7. Refrain from violence of fist, tongue or heart.

Taken together, it is fair to conclude from these principles that we should treat others with courtesy and respect. We should do our best to regard opponents, especially those who claim the same faith, not as enemies but as friends with whom we disagree.

Within two minutes of reading these words, however, Reed himself, in the authors' judgment, violated the spirit of this pledge in an aggressive political attack on the Clinton administration. He sarcastically dismissed as political posturing the President's then-recent statements of support for traditional values and for religious expression in public schools. He called attention to Clinton's 1992 statement that "sometimes the bully pulpit becomes the pulpit of bull."

He quickly moved on to lambaste the President for sending the First Lady to the United Nations Women's Conference in China "where forced abortion and infanticide committed against female babies is a mandatory national policy." He argued that this would "give credibility to one of the most brutal political regimes in the entire world."

For the record, how to deal with oppressive political regimes has long been debated by American politicians. It was the Nixon administration that normalized relationships with China, much to the dismay of some advocates of human rights. Can the United States exert more influence by boycotting or by furthering relations? Moral principles can be cited on both sides. Billy Graham faced this dilemma when he operated behind the Iron Curtain in the Cold War days. Ultimately, this is an issue of personal and political judgment. That Reed seized the moment to attack the President exemplifies his organization's essentially political character.

The principles from the pledge card imply that political opponents should be treated fairly. Ralph Reed has every right to disagree with the President's decision to send his wife to China. But in the authors' judgment, it was unfair of Reed not to mention what Mrs. Clinton said while she was there. She chastised this oppressive regime on its own turf more aggressively than any American spokesperson had ever done. Among her statements was the following: "It is a violation of human rights when women are denied the right to plan their own families, and that includes being forced to have abortions or being sterilized against their will."[7]

With this attack following so closely on the heels of the pledge, it is fair to wonder exactly what Reed means when he speaks of observing with friend and foe "the ordinary rules of courtesy." And if this is the example set by the leader, it is not surprising that some of the Coalition's followers forget that all people, even homosexual protestors, are created in the image of God.

The true character of the Christian Coalition was suggested in other ways at the 1995 Road to Victory conference. To the credit of conference organizers, several speakers offered sound advice regarding the attitudes and principles that should govern Christians' political activity. Many of the words appear as quotes that begin chapters throughout this book. In essence, they challenged those in attendance to put Christian principle before partisan politics, to treat opponents with respect, to shun arrogance, and to promote compassion. Said Congressman Charles Stenholm of Texas, "My only request is that you always take time to hear both sides of all of the issues and realize that good, constructive, helpful ideas can come from all points of view on the political spectrum." Said Arkansas Lieutenant Governor Mike Huckabee,

As Christians, let us understand that we can disagree without being disagreeable. Jesus, . . . our Standard-bearer, is not one who would encourage us to cynicism, but to citizenship. I do not believe he is one that would encourage us to heckle, to boo, to hiss, to be difficult and dissident, but rather to be people who are known by our love.[8]

If Coalition members would take this kind of advice seriously, perhaps they *would* come to be viewed more as servants of a humble carpenter from Galilee. Unfortunately, the speakers who offered what seemed to be words of correction were generally met merely with polite applause.

In contrast, the speaker who had the masses on their feet and worked into a frenzy was radio show host and publishing executive Star Parker. In her address, Parker called not for welfare reform but for the abolishment of the welfare system. She advocated the dismantling of public education, adding that if parents could not find a school for their children, they should educate them at home.

Parker called for an end to *all* government regulation of small business, contending that Jesus' parable of the talents in Matthew 25 establishes that "God is a capitalist." She called for the swift execution of "murderers, rapists, and kidnappers" and proposed that all other criminals be "shipped off" to one big prison facility.

The cassette tape of Parker's address went through several "printings" even before the conference ended. According to those operating the cassette booth, Parker's tape was the one most in demand with no close second. This is the kind of anecdote that challenges the contention that Coalition members represent America's mainstream. It feeds the perception of the Christian Coalition as a radical fringe.

Addressing issues politically instead of prophetically risks distorting what the church should be saying about various issues and problems. For example, in his conference address Christian Coalition founder Pat Robertson drew a thunderous applause when, addressing the topic of educational vouchers, he said, "If the Left thinks so highly of choice in regard to what you do with an unborn baby, how about giving us choice in regard to what we do with our teenagers."

The problem with this consistency argument is that it cuts both ways. According to Robertson's logic, if the Left would concede educational vouchers, Christians ought to concede to choice in the pro-life debate. Robertson's rhetoric makes for a great speech, but its implications are potentially dangerous for unborn children.

An occasional hymn or prayer was not enough to transform the essential character of the Road to Victory event, which bore a strong similarity to a political party convention. This is not what one would expect from a gathering of people committed first to Christ.

The name "Christian Coalition" no doubt makes political activity palatable for those fundamentalist Christians who are still outgrowing the belief that such activity is too worldly. This is a legacy from a previous generation of believers. For some, to label an organization as "Christian" justifies their participation by enabling them to believe they are involved in mission work, not politics.

A name, however, can change only perception, not reality. Thus, in response to the question, "Is the Coalition Christian?", we must answer, "Not very." To be sure, the overwhelmingly majority of its members are Christians. Most of them, no doubt, are well meaning people who, motivated by biblical values, have sacrificed their time, energy, and financial resources because they care about their families and country. The Coalition, and other organizations on the Christian Right, are contributing a valuable political perspective to the debate. But again, it is just that: a political perspective, one that is not intrinsically related to the primary mission of the church.

Furthermore, as argued above, the behavior and attitudes that permeate this organization owe more to the ground rules that govern politics than to the principles that should govern Christians. We will now examine why we consider this such a serious problem for the mission of the church.

Chapter Three

Preserving the Church's Unique Mission

I'm not afraid that we will take over the Republican Party.
I'm afraid the Republican Party ... may take us over.

Family Research Council President Gary Bauer at the
Christian Coalition's 1995 Road to Victory conference

Charles Colson's column "Plotting for the Presidency" in the June 19, 1995, issue of *Christianity Today* is a masterpiece. He writes of a dream that he's back in his White House days as a GOP strategist trying to make sure his party wins the presidency. Through lots of give and take, the small group eventually figures out a way to appease the pro-life movement while retaining its essentially pro-choice identity to keep moderates in the party happy.

One of those present at the meeting tries to stress the point that abortion is a moral issue. But in his dream, Colson cuts the guy off and says, "Politics is about winning. We have to get the power first. Then we can do what's right." He wakes up from his dream and prays, "Oh, Lord, what a nightmare. Thank you for taking me away from politics—and away from the political mentality of winning at any cost."

Having argued in the previous chapter that the primary identity of the Christian Coalition is political, we repeat that there is nothing inherently illegal or immoral about that. The problem is not that the Coalition is political, but that it is hesitant to acknowledge that it is. By holding itself up as "Christian," it confuses the important distinction between the church and the political realm. In so doing, it threatens to damage the church's credibility in the mission field of America and around the world. This critique applies to all organizations and leaders within the Christian Right who state or imply that their political conclusions are the only ones true believers ought to hold.

Virtually all Christians agree that the spiritual mission of the church is a far greater priority than the political mission of individual Christians or quasi-Christian organizations such as those that constitute the Religious Right. Among the 12 apostles Jesus chose were a tax collector (pro-government bureaucrat) and a Zealot (anti-government radical). This supports the view that Jesus' mission transcended political differences.

The late French theologian Jacques Ellul regularly urged Christians not to make politics paramount because it frequently leads to illusory "solutions." As Senator Dan Coats puts it, "Who we vote for as Christians is finally less important than who each of us is as a Christian. The ultimate source of our success is not our [political] organizational ability, but our faithfulness to a higher call."[1]

Evangelicals are distinguished in large part by their commitment to be ambassadors for Jesus Christ. The highest mission priority to most evangelicals is to bring others into a living relationship with God through Christ. That mission is compromised in the eyes of the world when people see the gospel linked to a particular political program. In a previous generation, this would have been a warning to Christians on the political Left. But in 1996, it is a caution to the Right.

Perhaps because of the association of ecumenism with liberalism, theologically conservative Christians have ignored the biblical injunction to pursue spiritual unity. We in America have perhaps drunk too deeply from the well of prosperity and political freedom. Persecuted Christians living in other lands tend to forget about denominational and political differences and to remember what and who unites them.

In contrast, despite a common faith, evangelicals today on the political Left and those on the political Right have, for the most part, little to do with one another. The gulf between them is at least as deep as—and probably deeper than—the gulf that separates ideological opponents in the society at large. Those on the Right seem to feel more at home with political conservatives of other religions or of no religion than they do with their evangelical brothers and sisters with whom they are at odds politically. On the other hand, some of the rhetoric that emanates from the evangelical Left similarly suggests that those at the opposite political extreme are ultimately enemies, not co-laborers for Christ and his kingdom.

Both the Left and Right question each other's intelligence, motives, and even sincerity of faith. Unable or unwilling to acknowledge ambiguity or uncertainty in their political judgments, they make no effort to find common ground or to recognize possible merit in the other's point of view. They talk *at* each other from a distance instead of *with* one another from up close. Apparently, the blood that runs through politics is thicker than the blood of Jesus Christ.

This is not to deny that the Bible speaks to social and political issues. But it is an undeniable fact that Christians in 1996 do not agree on how the Bible should be applied in the political arena. We can go on accusing the other side of being unspiritual, not very smart, or both. Or we can choose the moderate path by respecting each other despite differences and by affirming unity of faith for the sake of the church's greater mission.

Scripture's admonitions for visible unity are present for a purpose. They recognize the primacy of the church's spiritual mission as over against the political activities of individual believers. If the church does not present a moral witness that transcends politics, various wings of the church become nothing more than political interest groups at war with one another. Again, when that happens—and we believe it already has—the church's primary mission is at risk of being compromised or lost.

The church ought to inform *all* political viewpoints with moral considerations by upholding biblical principles without regard to political ideologies. The moral positions it upholds must not be determined by surveys revealing where the majority of citizens stand on any given issue. The church must stand apart from the world's disorder and violence in order to represent the ideal of a community bonded by faith, comprised of people from all races, nations, and classes who represent a variety of political perspectives.

The church of Jesus Christ is uniquely qualified to uphold moral principles based on the teachings of Scripture. If the church's mission in this regard is to remain pure, the question of *how* those principles ought to be translated into public policy must be left to the realm of politics. The church must avoid ordaining political philosophies or particular political viewpoints over which Christians—including those with identical theological perspectives—are divided.

To be sure, the Christian Coalition and other organizations of the Christian Right do not claim to speak as the church. But the perception that they do is understandable and inevitable when the Right suppresses—or denies the validity of—alternative political viewpoints held by other believers.

This analysis is nothing new. A similar phenomenon happened frequently during the Cold War, when the political pronouncements of mainline denominations were predictably and instinctively Left-leaning. Evangelical renewal groups, supported by the influential Institute on Religion and Democracy, argued justifiably that pronouncements of the corporate church should be limited to the expression of moral principles. Of course, the corollary was that the church should steer clear of specific domestic or foreign policy analysis and proposals, giving its individual members the freedom to reach their own conclusions on these matters.

In contrast to mainline denominations, the National Association of Evangelicals (NAE) has never strayed far from a "lowest common denominator" approach to public pronouncements. In the face of the criticism that it has rendered itself irrelevant by passing up opportunities to weigh in on social and political issues, the NAE has stayed the course, issuing statements only when the consensus among its constituents is unanimous or nearly so. It has done this for the important purpose of preserving a clear distinction between the church and the political realm.

These days, however, this distinction is at risk of being lost. In the minds of many Americans, the mission of the church has been equated with the mission of the Republican party's conservative wing. Whether intended or not, one major implication of the Christian Coalition's political activities has been to define Christian principles in terms of Republican political viewpoints.

At the Coalition's 1995 Road to Victory conference, Pat Robertson, the organization's founder, talked about the goals he had set in the early days: "I said we would have a significant voice—actually I said something else, but Ralph [Reed] said I can't say that here tonight because we got press—that we would have a significant voice in one of the political parties by 1994." Since the organization would not reveal to the authors what Robertson really said back in 1989, we can only speculate it had something to do with the organization's efforts to gain control of the Republican party.

The identification of Christianity with the political Right shows up even in bookstores. Last summer, one of the authors of this book visited several Christian bookstores in Atlanta that were well-stocked with books representing conservative political viewpoints. None of them had a copy of Jim Wallis's *The Soul of Politics,* which represents alternative political views. Most, however, did carry Rush Limbaugh's *The Way Things Ought to Be,* testifying to the growing number of "Rushian Christians" in the evangelical market. For evangelical Rushians, Limbaugh's staunch political conservatism apparently trumps his questionable stands on some moral and theological issues.

In contrast, Congressman Charles Stenholm told the Christian Coalition's 1995 Road to Victory conference, "I've been reading my Bible for fifty years, and I can't find any Party affiliation for Jesus." Stating that he was "far from alone" as a Democratic official who takes his Christian beliefs seriously, Stenholm expressed his concern about press reports suggesting that organizations such as the Christian Coalition receive their marching orders directly from Republican party headquarters. If those reports are false, he suggested that "greater missionary work and greater sensitivity to fellow Christian Democrats is in order." If the reports are true, he said, "I would suggest the inclusive name 'Christian' is not a proper title for a partisan organization."

Some church traditions have shunned political action based on the truth of the maxim, "Power corrupts." Christians who hold an orthodox view of the sinfulness of human nature certainly agree. But the nature of our sinfulness is such that we usually notice the corruptive capacity of power only in the lives of others. Power is not a problem as long as we are the ones who have it.

Those on the Christian Right who are now basking in the glow of their rediscovered political strength would do well to heed the warning of theologian Christopher A. Hall: "The dispiriting possibility exists that an evangelical vision for North American Society might ultimately come to fruition through engagement in the political process, with the great irony that we are incapable of incarnating that vision because of who we have become in the process of achieving our goals."[2]

If the church is to remain true to its mission—and if it is to be untainted by partisan politics—moderates and the political philosophy they represent must lead the way. That philosophy recognizes the complexity of the task of translating a wide array of biblical principles originally written for Christians who lived nearly two thousand years ago into public policy for twentieth-century America. Based on that recognition, moderates must approach this awesome task with fear, trembling, and a heavy dose of humility, recognizing that the purity of the church's mission, as well as its vitality in our society, is at stake.

We believe it is incumbent upon those who agree theologically to find a way to express their unity in faith despite their political differences. A critique of the Christian Right must go beyond mere criticism if the political gulf that divides the church is to be healed. While we question the wisdom of the Right's modus operandi, we must acknowledge the sincere motivation of many who are involved, especially at the grassroots level.

For some, this entails rejecting the stereotype of fundamentalists as redneck bigots who care only about themselves. Many of those who are a part of the Christian Coalition are responding to deep and legitimate fears and concerns about the moral climate of our culture. By and large, they are not people of great wealth or stature. They are ordinary people who have come into their power not by social privilege but by a long-term commitment to hard work. Their frustration with, and critique of, the system and the powers that be at many points parallels the critique of those on the political Left.

We must be careful not to equate the religious conservative with his distant cousin, the white supremacist, who continues to spew forth hatred in this country, albeit now on the fringes of society. Widely portrayed as narrow-minded, judgmental, selfish prudes, fundamentalists are mainly hard-working people who do not murder or steal, who love their families, and who attempt to treat others with dignity and respect. The case could be made that if everyone lived that way, the world would be a better place. Similarly, we must resist the stereotype of those on the Christian Left as being anti-American and anti-free market tree huggers who believe that government can solve all of the country's ills.

Although Christians on the Left and Right interpret the Bible differently, a shared commitment to the authority of Scripture can and ought to serve as the basis for striving toward spiritual unity. "The Ten Commandments of Moderate Political Behavior," presented in chapter 5, are intended to promote reasoned political discussion in the society at large. They also represent the hope for Christians with similar theological inclinations and bases for moral authority to present a unified moral witness to the world.

For the sake of the church's unique mission, we must learn to regard one another not as enemies, but as friends, even sisters and brothers, who disagree. Moderates who are true to their calling can locate such persons whether they are looking to the Left or to the Right.

The Reverend Jerry Falwell and U.S. Senator Ted Kennedy will almost certainly never vote for the same President or agree on a major public policy issue. But their animosity toward each other has been muted ever since their dinner together in the early 1980s. Political opponents, particularly Christians, can gain something from their example.

Chapter Four

The Pathology of Ideology

Polarization driven by individual interest and enforced by ceaseless negativism about our government is extremely unhealthy for the country.

Congressman Charles Stenholm of Texas at the
Christian Coalition's 1995 Road to Victory conference

In the first U.S. presidential election, the losing candidate, as runner-up, became vice-president. The thinking was that the candidates were ultimately on the same side. Political parties did not exist. They were not even mentioned in the Constitution. The nation's leaders agreed on the problems and issues the new country faced. The only thing left for the people was to decide which candidate was most capable of providing leadership.

Times have changed. Whether they've changed for better or worse is debatable. In times of national crisis, we get the ceremonial "We're all Americans" speech from both sides of the political aisle, but the rest of the time each side would have us believe that they alone know what is best for America. Both sides behave in ways that suggest that they believe they have cornered the market on political truth. Moderates explore the possibility that neither has.

To be sure, it is unfair to compare the political atmosphere of early America with that of today. Back then, a common enemy served to negate any philosophical differences that may have existed among potential leaders. They took Ben Franklin's advice to hang together in order to escape being hanged separately. What's more, the sociological and technological developments that gave rise to different political perspectives—developments such as women's liberation and industrialization—had yet to take place.

The emergence of fundamentally different ideas about how the nation should operate was inevitable. That these ideas would be expressed with such vitriol and contempt for political opponents—and without any acknowledgment of ambiguity—was neither inevitable nor necessary or helpful. These days some congressional members will not even stand and offer polite applause when the President enters the chamber.

Politicians routinely claim that they are not motivated by politics but rather by the desire to give the American people what they want. No politician would ever admit to being a political "ideologue." That's a pejorative they reserve for describing those who disagree. For example, the conservative Republicans' Contract with America was presented not as part of a political ideology, but as a 10-point list of what the majority of Americans wanted. To be sure, the Contract did overlap significantly with what surveys indicated most Americans indeed want. Yet the Contract called for increases in defense spending, even though that point does not command the support of the majority of Americans.[1] Why would the Contract's advocates not be consistent in giving Americans what they desire? Ideology. The Right has traditionally supported military preparedness. The majority of Americans may not agree, but most weapons manufacturers do.

The fact that campaign financing has so much to do with who gets elected also feeds the pathology of ideology. Candidates must be careful not to run afoul of the views of those who are paying for the TV commercials. By and large, that translates into sticking with the ideological program.

In addition, candidates' efforts to acquire or hold onto political power has to a large extent become a higher priority than the best interests of individual citizens and the nation as a whole. Nowhere is this more evident than in the predominance of career politicians. At the risk of compromising the nation's best interests, the career politician typically keeps a steady flow of political pork coming to his or her representative district in exchange for votes on Election Day.

The very concept of a career politician was foreign to the country's first political leaders. In an earlier era, political service to the nation was regarded as an obligation, not as an opportunity to become rich, powerful, or famous, or to satisfy an overgrown ego. In keeping with the principles of a citizen legislature, those who had the ability "did their time" and then returned to the farm to get on with life. Term limits did not have to be debated as a political issue. They were largely assumed. The fact that term limits was the only provision in the Contract with America that the House did not pass during 1995 should tell us something about politicians and their motives: Most of them favor term limits only when it's someone else's term.

The desperate hunger to get elected or reelected has fueled the evolution of "wedge politics," as opposed to political behavior rooted in civility, consensus, and the desire to solve the real problems faced by the world, this nation, and its citizens. In accordance with wedge politics, the candidate's modus operandi, as the name suggests, is to drive a wedge between himself or herself and the opponent in order to achieve as much distance as possible. The candidates then proceed to portray the other as incompetent, immoral, or both.

Despite candidates' rhetoric about sticking to the issues, we have in recent years witnessed the consistent degeneration of political campaigns at all levels into name-calling, stereotyping, and character assassination. This has the effect of destroying confidence in the system, as even the winning candidate ends up covered with mud that is hard to wash off.

Congressional wars over the appointments of Supreme Court

justices—let alone cabinet positions or a Surgeon General—were once unheard of. In today's political climate, such battles are routine. The 1995 Waco hearings, for example, could have been an opportunity to assess what the government did wrong and to determine how to avoid similar mistakes in the future. Instead, they served merely as an arena for Republicans to attack a Democratic administration. No doubt, had Waco taken place during a Republican administration, most congressional Democrats would have reached different conclusions about how the government handled it.

Except for an occasional debate on public television, the issues do not get addressed in any meaningful way. Contemporary political campaigns are designed from day one not to engage opponents in substantive dialogue but to motivate like-minded ideologues to get out and vote. The best way to do this is to strike terror into the hearts of voters at the expense of magnanimity and sometimes truthfulness. The media contribute to this atmosphere by reporting on campaigns as if they are horse races, mainly focusing on who is ahead and by how much.

In a two-party system such as ours, those operating out of a wedge political mentality find ideological wedges among the most convenient ones to drive. No doubt, many candidates are not extremist by nature. However, the system in which they are operating does not permit the freedom to struggle honestly with difficult issues, especially when that entails crossing ideological boundaries. To weigh difficult issues or to examine various alternatives is to come across as "wishy-washy" and to risk political suicide.

In order to succeed, especially as they move up the political ladder, candidates must associate with one political party or the other. They must guard against taking positions on major issues that cross ideological lines. Those who are naturally inclined to do so must at some point determine the issues on which to "flip-flop" in order to come into conformity. Such flip-flopping, while a political liability, is considered less risky than trying to bridge the ideologies. In today's political environment, it is a "necessary evil," the way the game is played.

Ideological battles in the strictly political realm reflect the severe polarization in the society at large. We gave up long ago trying to reason with or persuade others. We have opted instead for hardball politics. Our society's philosophical and political divisions have been enhanced by the unnecessary and unhelpful metaphors of war, as in "culture wars." Such characterizations merely feed the fires of animosity and bar the doors of minds to ensure they remain closed forever.

University of Virginia sociologist James Davison Hunter writes, "Philosophers and social scientists have observed that during times of social fluctuation and cultural uncertainty, communities may unwittingly exaggerate a threat to their existence and well-being. These communities under stress may even *fabricate* such a threat."[2]

In the midst of this intense cultural warfare we can all be thankful for the chance to experience some comic relief in the person of Rush Limbaugh, the king of conservative talk radio. Limbaugh is a study in contrasts: polite to his callers, cheerful, kind on a personal level, and eminently likable to most who give him half a chance. Yet some of his remarks and attitudes communicate insensitivity or even cruelty, putting him at or near the top of the Left's list of the most irritating conservatives.

Like all good satirists, Limbaugh suffers from being misunderstood. Those on the Left, especially, take him too seriously, far more seriously than he takes himself. No one would question Limbaugh's sincere conservatism, nor deny the validity of some his creatively expressed viewpoints. But we must understand that Rush Limbaugh is, at heart, an entertainer, and a good one at that. He has successfully carved out an image for himself as someone who is always right. In the same way that Rodney Dangerfield built a career out of getting no respect, Rush has been able to trade on his image, hawking crust-first pizza for Pizza Hut and appearing as his inimitable self on at least one television sitcom.

Unlike some of his followers, Rush knows that not everything he says or writes should be taken at face value. For example, when he wrote that George Bush changed his stance on abortion in the late 1970s because of the growing number of abortions—as if political expediency had nothing to do with it—Rush must have been chortling as he thought about the wackos who would take him seriously on this point.[3]

But if the Left takes Rush too seriously, so do many of those on the Right, including the aforementioned "evangelical Rushians." Those who love the humor—but don't get the satire—get a rush out of Rush. He affirms for them what they want to believe, gives them confidence, makes them feel good about themselves with the realization that they've been right all along. The net effect increases society's polarization.

The hunger for ratings among the media ultimately also feeds the society's tendencies toward extremist views. A hardened ideologue's black-and-white world can be contained in the kinds of sound bites journalists want. Moderates need a little more time to explain the subtleties of the issues. What's more, extremists are almost always more eccentric, and eccentricity is good for ratings.

Uncompromising ideology inevitably takes its toll on the kind of thorough dialogue and debate required for progress in a pluralistic society. It leads to the kinds of political games wherein one party tacks on a piece of legislation to another, totally unrelated piece, forcing legislators either to give up on legislation they wanted or vote for something they oppose. Thus, a decision-making process that is driven by ideology is deprived of integrity. The winners are not those with the best arguments, those who are closest to the truth. Instead the winners are those with the biggest or best political weapons, the smartest political ploys, the most expensive media campaigns, or the most efficient methods to get the votes needed, whether on Election Day or on the floor of the House.

Ideally, political leaders—and people in general—would consider each issue based on its own merits in the effort to make responsible decisions. In keeping with the principles of inductive reasoning, they would gather facts, examine trends, and consider various theories as well as public opinion before reaching an informed conclusion. And even then, the conclusion would be subject to revision based on new facts.

In contrast, when ideology reigns supreme, the process that takes place is more akin to deductive reasoning. That is to say that the conclusions are already in place. The effort to gather facts and solicit opinions is based not on the goal of reaching a conclusion but on the need to support a premature conclusion, which cannot be modified. If the devil can cite Scripture according to his purposes, politicians can and do cite facts that support their purposes. And advocacy organizations can word the questions in public opinions polls in ways that ensure they will get the answers they want.

The pathology of ideology ultimately can be traced to individuals who are the ones who form and participate in political parties. We challenge all persons to examine the extent to which they have become ideologues, perhaps without even realizing it. We challenge people to make an intentional effort to question their political presuppositions and to listen carefully to those who represent different political viewpoints. In order to break the chains of ideological captivation, we need more people who are willing to follow the path toward truth, even when it challenges ideas and beliefs they have long held dear.

The factors that contribute to the formation of an individual's political views are many, varied, and complex, so complex that often they are not readily apparent even to the individual. We arrive at different political perspectives for several reasons. First, God has created each of us with a distinct personality. Second, we have learned—whether we realize it or not—different political and social values from our parents, based, for example, on how they earned (or failed to earn) a living. Third, life itself has provided us with different experiences. A person who has been victimized by crime and another who has been falsely accused will inevitably embark on a discussion of the criminal justice system from different starting points. As the saying goes, a conservative is a liberal who's been mugged. President Reagan might never have spoken out in favor of the Brady Bill (advocating gun control) had he not been shot along with James Brady in 1981. Christians who live in the city generally have different viewpoints on the welfare system from those who live in the suburbs. As we move into adulthood, all these varied contributing factors merge to form a basic political perspective. Some can even cite the event, place, and time when "I became a Republican" or when "I realized I was a Democrat."

Like an amateur golfer's grip on a club, a political framework that has been formed tends toward inflexibility, even to the point of stubbornly rejecting good advice or new information. Instead of being allowed to press on the edges of the framework so that it can continue to form, facts and new experiences are forced into frameworks whose growth has been stunted prematurely.

The challenge that stands before evangelical moderates is to present and model an alternative. In part it entails support for candidates who, based on integrity, demonstrate the political courage necessary in this day and age to break away from a party's ideological lines. Most likely, many such candidates will go down in flames before a dent is made in the current system, but progress must begin somewhere.

Moderates should not disregard the possibility of organizing politically as those on the Right have done. What is most needed, however, is not another political organization, even one that breaks traditional ideological molds. Rather, we need a new process: a set of rules, principles, and attitudes designed to build understanding and promote mutual respect, even in the context of intense political and social rivalry. We need—in the church, in the political realm, and in the larger society—a process that enables us to diffuse the culture war and move toward more reasoned and patient discussion and debate.

We now invite the reader to turn with us to consider the principles and attitudes that comprise this process in our proposed "Ten Commandments of Moderate Political Behavior."

Chapter Five

The Ten Commandments of Moderate Political Behavior

If both sides were to spend more time seeking common ground rather than relishing the differences that can be capsulized into 15-second sound bites in next year's campaign, they would find a surprising amount of agreement to build on.

Congressman Charles Stenholm of Texas at the
Christian Coalition's 1995 Road to Victory conference

---

1. Thou shalt acknowledge thine own finite and sinful nature and, thus, the limited scope of thy perspective.

The Bible clearly teaches that, unlike animals, human beings bear the image of God. This theological affirmation establishes that human beings possess inherent dignity and are capable of reason. Yet the ways of God are beyond human comprehension. The gap between Creator and created humanity—Karl Barth called it the "otherness" of God—encompasses both our moral capabilities and our capacity for knowledge and understanding. God knows all things, can do all things, and is morally perfect. But the knowledge and capacity for moral judgment of even the wisest and most moral human being is both limited and even impaired because of our fallen nature.

Every time a prayer does not get answered in the way we hoped, we remind ourselves that God knows more about how to run the universe than we do. For some reason, however, this knowledge of our limitations does not seem to carry over into the political realm. Humility that acknowledges the possibilities of limited perspectives, self-serving interests, and flaws in our thinking seems noticeably absent from the public square.

Intellectually, everyone concedes that the answers to life's tough questions are not always clear and simple. Admitting such, however, violates the rules of political behavior, wherein being unsure about anything is viewed as a liability. We tend to elect leaders who have mastered the art of seeming certain, even when they aren't.

Alban Institute founder Loren Mead points out that polarities, by definition, are "differences you live with but never resolve." He adds that polarities are "particularly galling to religious people, who want a clearly defined 'right' and 'wrong.'" He points out that the church has historically struggled with tensions such as law versus grace, faith versus works, charismatic vigor versus ordered life, and flesh versus spirit. "If there is a lesson from this history," he writes, "it is that one is always tempted toward one of the poles, but that none of them is complete by itself."[1]

Part of the mystery and complexity of the Christian faith is that people of similar belief can arrive at different theological and political conclusions. Among the tasks of moderates is to recognize the assets and the liabilities—the strengths and the risks—of political positions on both ends of the political spectrum. Moderates are open to the possibility that deeper insight into the Christian faith might be found amidst political diversity.

In his book *The Scandal of the Evangelical Mind,* Mark Noll observes that intellectual life entails "a certain amount of self-awareness about alternative interpretations or a certain amount of tentativeness in exploring the connection between evidence and conclusions...."[2] In other words, truth is more evasive than politicos would like us to believe.

William Penn said that if something is true, it remains true no matter how many believe it to be false. We affirm that as a clear statement of absolute truth. But when sincere Christians disagree, Penn's advice does nothing to help us determine who is closer to the truth.

As moderates, we believe it is possible to have a strong opinion on an issue while at the same time recognizing the legitimacy of other perspectives. We affirm the reality of moral absolutes. But our capacity as humans to perceive absolute truth is imperfect. Paul reminds us that we see "through a glass darkly." We are limited by our finite nature and by the presence of sin in the world and in our lives. This does not mean we are incapable of perceiving or stating truth. Nor does it suggest that all perceptions of truth—whether religious or political—are equally valid, for that constitutes moral relativism. However, our efforts to persuade one another with regard to whose perception has greater validity must, in light of fundamental evangelical theology, be carried out with humility and respect, particularly in relation with fellow believers, who agree that the Bible is God's Word and thus the source of all truth.

Unfortunately, some will conclude from this that moderates are "wishy-washy," unwilling to take a stand. Moderates do take firm stands on fundamental moral issues. As with all Christians, we affirm that some behaviors and attitudes are clearly right and others are clearly wrong. But we are hesitant about making such absolute judgments when it comes to political issues where scriptural principles seem to compete with one another. Even in those cases, we encourage moderates to take a stand. We believe it is not only possible but necessary for people to hold passionately to their beliefs while acknowledging at the same time that they could be wrong, that they might change their minds, that they might some day have to seek forgiveness. Because of those possibilities, we encourage respect for those who, at least for the time being, have arrived at a different conclusion.

The capacity to choose to do good or evil lies at the very heart of what it means to be human. Those who take seriously the theological affirmation of our fallen human nature should instinctively be more tentative and thoughtful in the expression of political views, rather than more certain and strident. Those who are in a position to influence hundreds or thousands of people should be especially careful and humble in the exercise of their power and influence.

2. Thou shalt acknowledge that thy brother or sister may disagree with thee and yet remain deserving of thy respect as a brother or sister.

Despite the belief that we are saved only through faith in Christ, followers of Christ both on the political Left and the Right are prone to question the legitimacy of others' faith based on their political and social beliefs and behaviors. Those on the Left find genuine faith in Christ incompatible with membership at a certain country club or with support for abolishing the welfare system. Meanwhile, some on the Right cannot conceive of a truly Christian church that would dare open its doors to a practicing homosexual or oppose organized prayer in public schools.

The most heated political rivalries often take place among those of common religious faith. For example, when those who claim to be Christians are at odds politically, both sides tend to accuse the other of abandoning the true faith. In contrast, when Christians disagree with atheists it comes as no surprise, since atheists don't claim to stand for Christian truth.

As stated in chapter 3, one of the scriptural principles we fail to take seriously is the admonition to pursue unity. To be sure, there must be some basis for unity, but again that basis is spiritual and theological in nature, not political. It is one thing to oppose another person's political conclusions or peripheral theological views based on one's reading of Scripture. But to judge the legitimacy or sincerity of a political opponent's faith is a different matter.

Although he is not as well known as Luther or Calvin, sixteenth-century theologian Philip Melanchthon is widely regarded as one of the Reformation's primary architects. Referred to by scholars as the "quiet Reformer," Melanchthon played a key role in developing the Reformation theology of Lutheranism, Methodism, Presbyterianism, and Anglicanism. He was also very heavily into palm reading and astrology. Should that disqualify this man, one of the most important contributors to evangelicals' religious heritage, from the ranks of Christianity? If not, then neither should political views deemed unbiblical serve as the basis for assessing the reality of another's faith. Christians are those who believe that Jesus Christ died for their sins and who accept him as their Savior.

When it comes to contemporary politics, we should be open to the possibility of truth coming from all points on the political spectrum. On some issues, elements of truth may come from both sides. On other issues, some may be right while others are wrong. Christians have every right and responsibility to argue their positions with confidence and vigor. We must, however, stop short of placing others outside of the kingdom or outside of God's will based on their political views. And we must fight through as many of our differences as possible for the sake of achieving spiritual unity.

3. Thou shalt learn to articulate fairly, honestly, and thoroughly the positions of thy opponent.

A common technique of marriage counselors is to have one spouse repeat what the other has just said in order to make sure each of them is listening carefully and understanding completely. The same principle would serve us well in the public square.

Sometimes we disagree with one another because of legitimate differences in analysis or perspective. Other times, however, the disagreement owes more to incorrect or incomplete understanding, resulting sometimes from irresponsible characterizations of the opponents' positions.

If a person truly believes that his or her argument is stronger than the opponent's, that person should have no reservations about representing the opponent's positions as accurately, fairly, and completely as possible. Not to do so betrays a lack of confidence in one's own position.

Being able to articulate an opponent's position presumes the willingness to become familiar with it. It means making a sincere effort to understand another's views and the ideas and experiences that have formed those views. The best way to do that is to interact with opponents civilly and compassionately, in full recognition of their humanity and the reality of their experiences and feelings.

With some issues, the debate entails technical or scholarly arguments. Just because lay persons are not scholars does not mean they are not entitled to opinions in these areas. It is perfectly legitimate for someone to draw a political or theological conclusion based on the knowledge that this position is supported by the scholars he or she trusts the most. We encourage as many as possible, however, to come to their own conclusions regarding what the Bible has to say or what public policy positions are best supported by biblical principles.

Finally, being fair to the other side entails telling the whole story, not just the part that suits one's purposes.

4. Thou shalt follow the path toward truth even when it challenges thy previous conclusions and beliefs.

Popular theologian R. C. Sproul, a die-hard Pittsburgh Steelers fan, was once asked if he could theologically justify his enjoyment of sports. He answered, "Yes, I can, but I should warn you I can make a theological justification for anything I like."

Much truth is spoken in this jest. Instead of allowing the Scriptures to challenge our ideas and convictions, it is easy to interpret the Bible in ways that confirm what we have always believed or what we want or need to believe. Desiring a cheap labor force, for example, early American businessmen interpreted the Bible in ways that justified chattel slavery.

For years, Prison Fellowship founder Charles Colson argued against capital punishment. In 1995 he revealed that he had changed his perspective. Though some might like his old position better than his new one, he at least deserves credit for being open-minded enough to be persuaded by new perspectives and arguments.

As noted earlier, an ideology serves the positive purpose of providing a framework within which to interpret facts and experiences. But a commitment to an ideology becomes a poor master when the framework becomes so rigid and inflexible that new information and experiences are not permitted to make even minor adjustments to the ideology itself. Hardened ideologues do not want to be bothered by facts that call their conclusions into question. They typically either ignore such facts or they sacrifice principles of integrity and logic in explaining them away.

This is sinful human nature at work. After years of deeply held beliefs, no one likes to admit that they may have been wrong. Nevertheless, hard as it might be, we must be willing to bring to light facts and perspectives that may force us to make adjustments to what we thought we knew for certain.

To state that theological and political beliefs should be grounded in Scripture is a helpful starting point. Unfortunately, all that means to many people is that they can believe anything for which they can find a verse or two somewhere in the Bible that seems to support their position.

Evangelicals are defined in large part by a high view of the authority of the Scriptures as God's unique Word for humankind. However, the flippant way many Christians use the Bible to support their arguments belies high respect for God's Word. For example, the common practice of "proof texting" is unreliable at best and abominable at worst. It constitutes severe ignorance with regard to how the Bible is meant to be understood and applied. This is not to say that citing a portion from Scripture to support an argument is always wrong. It is wrong, however, when Scripture is taken out of context and thus portrayed to mean something it was never intended to mean.

Evangelical hermeneutical theory stresses understanding the messages of the Bible as they were intended by the original authors to their original audiences. Grasping those messages entails an appreciation for literary forms and knowledge of the historical, cultural, social, and political contexts in which the authors functioned.

Many believers can't even name the languages in which the Bible was originally written, let alone appreciate the fact that some cultural differences are virtually "untranslatable." If most Christians had even a cursory appreciation for the kinds of considerations that go into Bible translations, our "conclusions" would be far less conclusive and far more open to revision in light of advances in scholarship.

Robert Wuthnow observes that "evangelicals are generally devout, church-going Christians who take the Bible seriously and try to live in obedience to their Lord. But study after study shows that they seldom understand the Bible very well, know little about theology, buy heavily into the therapeutic culture of 'feel-good-ism,' and are caught up in a cycle of overspending and consumption like everyone else."[3] Biblical ignorance is reflected in part by a 1994 Barna Research Group poll according to which one-fourth of respondents calling themselves "born-again Christians" believe Christ committed sins.[4]

Unfortunately, some conservative Christians typically mistrust scholarship, instinctively resisting new ideas that call into question traditionally held views. We must remember that it was a misuse of the Bible that allowed people to affirm that the black race was born out of the curse of Ham. It was a sounder hermeneutic—one that ceased regarding the Bible as a scientific textbook—that challenged the church to stop burning at the stake people who argued that the earth revolved around the sun. And it was enlightened biblical interpretation that challenged the use of 1 Timothy 6:1–6 to justify slavery.

As evangelicals, our primary basis for authority is neither reason nor experience nor tradition. Although relevant, all of these ultimately submit to the authority of Scripture. This means that from time to time we may have to reevaluate long-held and cherished beliefs. We cannot do or believe things simply because that is what we have always done and believed. We must be open to change, to new vistas of understanding. Otherwise, those who insist that the earth revolves around the sun would still be considered heretics.

We would all do well to heed the words of Gretchen Gaebelein Hull: "One of the saddest things about the dead hand of tradition is that it stifles discussion and encourages the closed mind. The person with the closed mind says, 'We've always done things this way. We have no new thing to learn.'"[5] What a tragedy!

Certainly, tradition has positive features. It provides a helpful reference point, one that serves to unify. Tradition helps us understand who we are today in light of who we have been. But tradition is dynamic. It should serve, not limit. It must be enriched with new understandings of how God is working in the world and through the church. The story of which we all are a part has not ended. Through healthy open-mindedness, we allow the story to continue.

5. Thou shalt encourage independent thinking rather than conformity, seeking to educate before seeking to persuade.

Some in the secular media contend that evangelicals and fundamentalists are mere foot soldiers in the culture war. A few years ago, the *Washington Post* described Christian conservatives as being "poor, uneducated and easy to command."[6] At its 1995 Road to Victory conference, Ralph Reed boasted about how the *Post*'s fax machines were tied up for three days by conservatives transmitting their 1040 Forms ("We're not poor") and their diplomas ("We're not uneducated"). Reed did not address the easy-to-command part.

As Mark Noll observes, "the evangelical ethos is activistic, populist, pragmatic, and utilitarian. It allows little space for broader or deeper intellectual effort because it is dominated by the urgencies of the moment."[7] That's a respectable scholar's gentle way of saying, "Evangelicals, taken together, tend to act before they think and fire before they aim."

The evangelical subculture has repeatedly displayed through the years its propensity for thoughtlessness. Squelching rumors in this subculture is like trying to blow out trick birthday candles. Through the years those rumors have included that Madalyn Murray O'Hair has filed a petition with the FCC to put an end to Christian broadcasting, that Procter & Gamble's logo is Satanic, and that Satanists are praying for the dissolution of Christian marriages.

Such a mentality is ripe for exploitation. All some media ministries and Christian organizations need to do is say the word and the phone lines at the White House get jammed or Congress gets flooded with letters. Analysis of the issues is typically one-sided, intended primarily to motivate people to action rather than encourage them to think, reach their own conclusions, and then respond as they deem appropriate. Given the divisions among evangelicals on many of these issues, we question whether this is an appropriate or responsible use of influence.

The evangelical ethos is also driven by publishers who care more about making profits than telling the truth. Noll points out that the flood of end-times books that became best sellers during and after the Persian Gulf War were based on a hermeneutic that "no responsible Christian teacher in the history of the church ever endorsed before this century came to dominate the minds of American evangelicals on scientific questions."[8]

That same, questionable hermeneutic, according to which the contemporary state of Israel will be at the center of the supposedly future events described in the book of Revelation, accounts for conservatives' instinctive and unconditional support for the state of Israel, support that typically casts broader issues of fundamental justice aside. To many fundamentalists, Israel remains God's chosen nation today. Such a view is reflected in the words of Ralph Reed: "We are the best friends that the Jews and the state of Israel ever had and we will never retreat from our love for the Jewish people and the state of Israel."[9]

Evangelical scholars have not reached a consensus regarding the role of contemporary Israel in end-times events. Some maintain that Israel has no special significance, emphasizing that the new Israel with which God has a unique relationship is not the Middle Eastern nation, but the church of Jesus Christ. Regardless of the differences of biblical interpretation, a substantial number of evangelicals oppose granting Israel preferential treatment. In a *Christianity Today* readership survey, 88 percent said that "Christians should hold the state of Israel to the same standards of justice and human rights in its international and internal affairs as any other nation."[10]

Christian leaders and organizations have a responsibility to resist exploiting evangelical foot soldiers' proclivity to unconsidered action. We question the extent to which they accept that responsibility. In order to maintain their tax-exempt status, politically minded nonprofits can avoid paying taxes as long as they focus on education rather than advocacy. Typically, these organizations abide by the letter of this law while forgetting the spirit. For example, they do surveys and then "educate" us all on the results. They know, however, that they can guarantee the results they want by the wording of the survey questions.

Unfortunately, most political activist organizations are not as interested in getting people to think as they are in getting people to take action or donate money.

6. Thou shalt seek to understand and acknowledge how thine own presuppositions, biases, and personal experiences may influence thy perspectives on various issues.

Alleging on his radio program that the federal education program Goals 2000 is an effort to indoctrinate young people in ways that demean America, James Dobson said, "We're biased on this, but this is what we think." Recognizing bias is a sign of maturity, but such recognition does no good, as in this case, if it is not allowed to inform political conclusions.

In essence, a bias is an unjustified feeling or belief. Being able to recognize and get beyond our biases constitutes one of life's toughest challenges. What we believe is right or wrong should be based on what the Bible teaches. Unfortunately, many of our feelings and beliefs owe more to cultural values or to what we were taught as youngsters. Those feelings can nevertheless be very strong and difficult to overcome.

Because most people are unaware of their bias, moving beyond bias entails a conscious effort to evaluate our moral judgments in the light of Scripture. Many people who are alive today were taught as youth that interracial dating was sinful. (Some fundamentalist schools still forbid it.) Such persons face the challenge of overcoming their feelings in the light of a more responsible interpretation of biblical teaching on race.

In the political debate, it is entirely possible for two people to agree totally on the facts surrounding a particular public policy issue and yet disagree on policy recommendations. This happens because we interpret and analyze the facts in the context of our experiences and our theological, social, and political perspectives, all of which may contribute to bias.

We need to examine our political viewpoints and conclusions in the full light of how they have been influenced by our past experiences. We can do this in part through self-reflection, making an intentional effort to understand how what we have experienced has helped formulate political views. We can also do it by listening to others, especially friends whose motives we trust. After all, political perspectives are influenced largely by what we believe about the way the world works and about human nature. Those beliefs are conditioned by such factors as family upbringing and unusual life experiences.

For example, some poor people might instinctively oppose welfare reform because their parents taught them to oppose anything that rich people support. Someone who has had only negative experiences with public schools is bound to be more likely to advocate educational vouchers. People who have lost friends or relatives to handguns are more likely to take a stand against the National Rifle Association (NRA). Someone who hails from a military family is likely to have a different perspective on America's use of the atom bomb than someone who grew up on the mission field in Japan. And pastors whose sons announce they are homosexual tend to view the gay issue in a different light.

That our experiences influence our political views may sound like a truism, yet most people have only a surface awareness of the significant factors that contribute to their political viewpoints. By examining our own experiences, and by listening to others whose experiences differ from our own, we can come to a greater appreciation of how we—and others—have arrived at political conclusions. Even if this process does not result in us changing our conclusions, at least it keeps us from raising them to the level of absolute truth. This process, we believe, is indispensable in the effort to move toward political behavior that is based on civility, mutual understanding, and consensus.

7. Thou shalt resist the temptation to stereotype and shalt instead realize that generalities often mask important distinctions.

Ideologues are drawn to stereotypes like proverbial moths to the flame: "the media is liberal"; "fundamentalists are bigoted"; "people on welfare are lazy"; "conservative Republicans are greedy capitalists"; or "television evangelists are crooks."

These are just some of the oft-stated but reckless convictions held by the ideologues among us. Unfortunately, the list could go on and on and on. Christians are just as guilty as their secular counterparts in succumbing to the urge to stereotype.

Stereotypes serve the convenient purpose of defining enemies in ways that make them easy to attack. They feed into ideologues' tendencies to characterize opponents as extremists, short-circuiting processes that might yield the conclusion that opponents, taken together, are not as far Left or Right as we would like them to be for fund raising purposes.

Some—perhaps most—stereotypical statements have some basis in truth; however, to advance oversimplified conclusions—whether actively or passively—as being categorically true is ultimately deceitful. They serve to polarize, rather than unite.

No one likes to be put into a category that defines the entirety of one's personality and values. It can be painful and frustrating when others conclude that we must think a certain way or believe certain things based on such factors as church tradition, economic status, or skin color.

Stereotyping prevents us from making the kinds of distinctions that are necessary in order to deal with the subtleties of issues. It results in the formation of negative images in the minds of people that can remain even long after change has taken place. For example, the city of Pittsburgh retains its image as a city of smokestacks even though it has gone hi-tech.

We can counteract this tendency to stereotype through a conscious effort to make specific statements rather than generalizing. We can do this, for example, by citing specific examples of liberal media bias or the materialism of conservatives without rushing to judgment on an entire class of people.

8. Thou shalt recognize, in this pluralistic nation, the important difference between shaping public policy based on Christian values and instituting public policy that is specifically Christian.

In some countries around the world, the presence or absence of values in the society depends in large part on whether the particular dictator in power happens to be benevolent. In the United States of America, political and individual freedom can and do coexist with moral values, including values derived from the Scriptures.

Each generation faces the task of considering the public policies according to which these two important priorities—freedom and values—can continue to find expression. People on both sides of the church-state debate regularly dispute whether the pendulum has swung too far in one direction or the other.

This issue will be considered more fully in chapter 7. For now, we merely state that this eighth commandment should serve as a fundamental principle in guiding moderate behavior in the public square as it relates to church-state issues. Christians must take great care as they operate in the political realm to distinguish between advocating moral principles based on their faith and advocating policies that wrongly deprive others of religious freedom. This affirmation stands in opposition to the stated views of some evangelicals, especially Christian Reconstructionists, who advocate a theocracy based on Old Testament law.

In addition to self-avowed and practicing theocrats, such as Gary North, Rousas John Rushdoony, David Chilton, and Joseph Morecraft, we will argue in chapter 6 for the existence of a category of conservatives who might be called "functional theocrats." These are people who do not want to institute Old Testament laws, but would not mind seeing a few specifically Christian principles made into law.

9. Thou shalt make a special effort to consider the viewpoints of those who, based on educational specialty or personal proximity, may have greater insight or a more informed perspective than the average citizen.

Common sense tells us that if we want to know why the car sounds funny, we should consult a mechanic, not a foot doctor. Such common sense, however, does not always carry over into the public policy decision-making process, which typically owes more to political pragmatism than to fairness and understanding of the facts.

Ideologues are naturally inclined toward accepting viewpoints that confirm their own beliefs rather than listening objectively to those in the best position to provide insight into a particular issue or topic. As a matter of principle, we should pay special attention to those who have the best access to the facts that inform public policy decisions. For example, not only do police officers have the most to lose from a bad policy on gun control, but they are in a good position to offer advice as to which policy might best accomplish society's goals. Their perspectives should be weighed more heavily than the perspectives of those looking on from a distance. This is not to suggest that those closest to the situation are always right, since close proximity can have a distorting effect on the larger picture. But as a matter of course, their views should be heard and considered seriously.

Of course, the corollary to this principle is that we should be more skeptical about accepting the conclusions of those who are not in the best position to know. Says evangelical missiologist and city dweller Ray Bakke, "It is very difficult for many solidly evangelical, mission-minded folk like me to trust people who convene in nearly all-white, privileged communities like Colorado Springs or safe suburbs, then from that place of safety and privilege come back to tell us how to vote and raise our children."[11]

Barbra Streisand is one of a number of Hollywood stars who have spoken out on moral and social issues. But does excellence as a performer and entertainer alone qualify a person to influence public policy?

Larry Burkett is an expert on financial planning. But in his book *Whatever Happened to America,* he takes on environmental isssues, categorically dismissing as myths what some consider to be serious environmental concerns, such as ozone depletion, the greenhouse effect, and overpopulation. His source of authority for these statements in his book is a publication of the John Birch Society.

James Dobson, the founder of Focus on the Family, is widely regarded—and deservedly so—as a landmark thinker and communicator in the area of child rearing and family life from a Christian perspective. Even many of those who disagree with his political views acknowledge that his contributions to helping families become healthy are incalculable. But is his political analysis as reliable as his psychological analysis? Millions of American Christians think so. They may be absolutely right. But people should not reach that conclusion based on his stature as a family psychologist and effective communicator.

10. Thou shalt, when in doubt, risk erring on the side of the most vulnerable.

Upon examining difficult issues, moderates are more inclined to see gray rather than black and white. Thus, the choice is often not between what is clearly right or wrong. Instead, in the absence of certainty, the decision is based on comparing the risks of being wrong on one side or the other.

As a matter of biblical principle, we believe that ethically ambiguous issues must be resolved in favor of those people who are most at risk. We acknowledge that the very effort to determine who is most vulnerable can itself be morally ambiguous, but we uphold this principle nonetheless as being helpful in resolving some ethical dilemmas related to public policy.

In 1989, James Dobson called attention to this kind of ethical dilemma in the context of the problem of abortion at Christian colleges. On his radio show, Dobson contended that the strict disciplinary policies of colleges in regard to out-of-wedlock pregnancies had the effect of driving young women to abortion, which Dobson considered to be a greater evil.[12] We agree. Calling attention to the policies of Christian colleges in this instance constituted a perfect example of erring on the side of the most vulnerable, namely, the unborn.

In 1995, the Family Research Council (FRC) faced a similar decision about its position on the provision of financial aid to women on welfare who became pregnant. Helen Alvare, a pro-life activist with the U.S. Catholic Conference, and former Pennsylvania Governor Robert Casey are among those who are convinced that women do not get pregnant in order to get more money and that this policy would have the effect of driving them toward abortion. The FRC's Gary Bauer acknowledged a difference of opinion among pro-life leaders but favored denying the aid. In contrast to Dobson, he was willing to take the chance that denying aid would help to create a moral climate over the long haul that would militate both against abortion and out-of-wedlock pregnancies.

Along with Alvare, Casey, and Dobson, we side with those who chose to risk erring in favor of those who are most vulnerable and most immediately at risk: unborn children.

This principle has a corollary: When difficult decisions must be made, you must take steps to minimize the potential fallout that results from the road not taken. Consider, for example, a choice between protecting an animal species and saving jobs. The fallout of a decision to save the animal species can be minimized by providing job training for those who are unemployed as a result of the decision.

Last year Congress debated a legislative provision introduced by U.S. Senator John Ashcroft of Missouri that proposed giving faith-based service organizations the opportunity to receive government funds without compromising their religious beliefs. Out of concern for religious freedom, the bill included a clause mandating the government to provide other service options for those uncomfortable with religious groups. That is a perfect example of addressing the concerns of those who feel that charitable groups should receive no government funds at all.

Like the original Ten Commandments, many of the principles of the "Ten Commandments of Moderate Political Behavior" can be summarized by the Golden Rule. In the public square, we should do our best to treat others with the same dignity and respect with which we would like to be treated. We do not intend these commandments to be exhaustive. We do believe that collectively they represent a starting point from which we can move toward more principled and reasoned debate. In the next section, we will attempt to apply the principles stated or implied by the commandments to some of the social and political issues facing the nation.

Part Two

INTRODUCTION

Once upon a time a man robbed a bank. Fortunately, two independent eyewitnesses saw him. One of the witnesses stood six feet five inches tall, had short-cropped hair, and was lean as a rail, while the other was a mere five-feet five, overweight, and had hair down to his shoulders. The guy who robbed the bank was the perfect median of the two witnesses: average height and weight, with medium-length hair.

The first eyewitness identified the robber as "a short, fat guy with long hair." The second said the villain was "tall and skinny with short hair." Based on this testimony, the police arrested both of the eyewitnesses, and the bank robber got away.

The moral of this fictional story is that we tend naturally to perceive, interpret, and describe reality from a particular perspective. Like the bank robber in the story, those who stand in the middle run the risk of being misperceived. After all, from the vantage point of a person standing all the way to one side, someone in the middle looks a lot like he's standing on the other side. Anyone who has ever officiated a basketball game knows how easy it is to be despised by both sides—simultaneously—despite one's best efforts to be fair and impartial.

We suspect that readers will both agree and disagree with much of our analysis of the issues in this section. We do not pretend that our treatment of the issues is exhaustive or even thorough. After all, many books have been written exclusively on each of the subjects we have chosen to address. Many readers, we suspect, will be frustrated both with what we have included and with what we have omitted in addressing these "hot-button" issues. But again, our primary goal is not to offer conclusive analysis, but to illustrate how our principles for moderate political behavior might find application. We don't want to end the debate, but rather begin a newer, better one.

That is not to say that we reach no conclusions at all or make no judgments regarding political positions of the Right and Left. It would be impossible to illustrate our "Ten Commandments" without making some preliminary judgments and drawing some general conclusions. But it should be noted that the authors themselves disagree with each other on the details of public policy recommendations. What we do agree on are the principles according to which we should conduct ourselves as Christians in a pluralistic democracy.

Most of the chapters in this section begin with a brief overview of each issue, followed by a moderate perspective. Because we agree with the maxim, "Dogma divides; mission unites," we have concluded each chapter with a section called "Points of Unity," that is, things all evangelicals ought to be able to affirm and work toward together despite their political differences.

We hope that the following insights into many of the most hotly debated issues of our time will increase understanding of the principles for appropriate political behavior set forth in chapter 5. We believe that as people understand and attempt to apply these principles to the political debate, they will not only improve themselves as individuals, but will do what is best in the long run for our communities, our nation, and our world.

Chapter Six

The American Experiment

We have much to repent of for our treatment
of Indians and other minorities.

Peter Marshall at the Christian Coalition's 1995 Road to Victory conference

Political conservatives and liberals alike keenly understand the importance of history. They know that who we are today as a nation is determined to a large extent by who we were in the beginning and have been over the last two centuries. History is a largely subjective endeavor. Historical interpretation owes at least as much to the political motives of the interpreters as it does to documented facts.

Not surprisingly, extremists on both sides of the political fence have reached radically different conclusions regarding the motives and principles that brought this nation into being. Rush Limbaugh no doubt speaks for millions of Americans when he writes, "I don't give a hoot that [Christopher Columbus] gave some Indians a disease that they didn't have immunity against. We can't change that, we're here. We're the best country on earth and I'm sick and tired of people trying to change history so as to portray this country as an instrument of evil."[1]

A book published by the Council on Interracial Books for Children, Inc., reaches some different conclusions. It maintains the following:

1. Basic human rights—of life, liberty and the pursuit of happiness—have been denied to various groups throughout United States history.[2]
2. We see the Revolution of 1776 as—among others things—a step in achieving greater social justice for *one* group of people—white males.[3]
3. The central fact at the core of the European advance was invasion and conquest.[4]

Those on the Left remind us of our forefathers' materialistic drive, pursued at the expense of the enslavement of one race and the near extinction of another. They emphasize the "might makes right" mentality that characterized early America, where brute force prevailed over reason and where the man with the quickest fists or the most accurate aim was deemed most likely to succeed.

Those on the Right paint a different picture, emphasizing the first Americans' bravery and courage in their efforts to get out from under an oppressive British regime. They call attention to the guiding principles of the founding fathers as expressed in the Declaration of Independence and the Constitution. Among those principles were the radical and visionary ideas of political and religious freedom, liberties we take for granted today. Conservatives also contend that the founding fathers were spiritual men, guided by prayer, belief in God, and principles of law and morality derived from a Judeo-Christian ethic.

A MODERATE PERSPECTIVE

We maintain that an evaluation of historical facts uninfluenced by uncompromising ideological commitment would reveal that both sides are right ... and wrong. A balanced examination, we believe, would reveal that this nation's founders were driven by a variety of motives. Then, as now, the society was far from monolithic. Some of our forefathers' attitudes and actions are worthy of our highest praise, while others deserve our most severe condemnation.

James Skillen of the Center for Public Justice points out that both the Christian Right and its most vociferous critics claim to be the true guardians of this nation's defining values. He calls America's moral-cultural unity an "increasingly murky myth."[5] We agree. Those who glorify the founders of the United States, making only ceremonial concessions to their shortcomings, would do well to take a closer look. Then, as now, this was a pluralistic society both in terms of religion and morality. Some of the founding fathers were ardent Christians and demonstrated it with their lives. Some used Christianity in ways convenient to meeting their larger social or political purposes. Still others openly rejected Christian truth. Enough of these religiously and morally diverse people were sufficiently united by the desire to create a nation that they were able to make it happen.

Some of the founding fathers would no doubt be unwelcome today in many of the same churches that regard them as heroes. For example, Ben Franklin was drunk during some of the Constitutional Convention, causing James Madison to go to great pains to ensure that Franklin did not talk to the press. According to some scholars, Thomas Jefferson, who rejected Christianity in favor of deism, fathered several illegitimate children. George Washington spoke of "Providence" but never of God or Jesus Christ. (None of this means that these men's great contributions to the nation should be ignored.)

Native Americans

Like their early American counterparts, contemporary ideologues arrive at different moral judgments with regard to the treatment of American Indians. To the Left, our treatment of Native Americans virtually defines this nation's moral character. Those on the Right would have us believe that our treatment of the Indians constitutes only a minor blip on America's laudable moral screen.

Through the years, Native Americans have been characterized by various groups as being peace-loving people on the one hand and savages on the other. Such generalized conclusions presume that Native Americans were monolithic. In fact, more than 400 Indian nations and tribes once inhabited what is now the United States and Canada.[6] By and large they got along with one another peacefully, but intertribal violence was by no means nonexistent, and when it happened, the victors were not beyond humiliating their enemies in dehumanizing ways.[7]

Some Native Americans were hospitable and friendly toward newcomers from Europe while others were less welcoming. Likewise the new settlers came with different ideas regarding how to treat the Indians. Some regarded them as savages and were prepared to shoot long before seeing the whites of their eyes. Others treated Indians with the kind of dignity and respect that should be given to all of God's people. Jonathan Edwards fought for the rights of Native Americans, even if it meant taking the local government to task. From the pulpit, he berated New England for having "debauched [the Indians] with strong drink instead of seeking their spiritual welfare."[8]

Christians have much to learn from the ways in which Native Americans in general cared for the Creation. Their respect for the land and for all creatures should have been a model for those who came from Europe. We should be able to emulate that respect without accepting the religious views on which it was based. Yet we must take care not to romanticize Native Americans' love for the land. Dale and Sandy Larsen point out that this "love" could be bought for the right price: "Native American respect for 'brother beaver' paled in the light of the white man's trinkets, knives, and blankets.... While whites provided the market, in the early days it was the Indians who provided the pelts."[9]

Nevertheless, we cannot deny that one result of European colonization was the destruction of entire nations and civilizations. Much of this was unintended: the result of smallpox, typhoid, measles, and other diseases for which Native Americans had no tolerance. But the abuse is also attributable to a philosophy of

European cultural superiority that justified treating red-skinned people as subhumans. However we qualify that by citing the belief systems out of which our forefathers were operating, all Americans today should be able to acknowledge in retrospect that our treatment of Native Americans constitutes a profound moral tragedy.

This kind of analysis stands in stark contrast to the portrayals of Indians in movies and television westerns of earlier eras, including the '50s, the conservatives' Golden Age. Most of us grew up believing that cowboys were always the heroes, the Indians were always the bad guys, and black people did not exist. Only in recent years has this stereotype been challenged by such films as *Dances With Wolves* and *Pocahontas* and by television shows such as *Dr. Quinn, Medicine Woman*.

Slavery

No responsible person would deny that the institution of slavery represents a colossal stain on the integrity of the founding fathers. We must be careful, however, not to paint all the founders with the same broad brush. Support for slavery was far from unanimous. For many, the issue of slavery presented a painful dilemma. They were morally opposed to it, but felt forced to compromise their morality for the sake of what they considered a larger cause: giving birth to a nation. We should remember that less than 90 years after this nation was born, hundreds of thousands of white Americans gave their lives in a war fought in large part over the issue of slavery.

Such observations can only qualify—they can never excuse—the moral abomination of slavery. We must work to go beyond viewing it merely as an unfortunate mistake in our past and instead acknowledge its relevance for evaluating the moral character of early America. Some have argued that seventeenth- and eighteenth-century behavior should not be judged by twentieth-century standards. They point out that the belief systems out of which people operated were based on ignorance. Some sincerely believed that conquering blacks and Indians was in keeping with God's will.

Let us not kid ourselves, however, with regard to how the mentality of white superiority originated. It was not apparent from "natural law." Rather, it arose·out of the economic "need" for cheap labor. Many people back then could see this as clearly as we see it today. For example, referring to slavery in the Caribbean, John Wesley wrote two years before the American Revolution that

> all those islands should remain uncultivated forever; yea, it were more desirable that they were altogether sunk in the depth of the sea, than that they should be cultivated at so high a price as the violation of mercy, justice, and truth; and it would better that none should labor there, that the work should be left undone, than that myriads of innocent men should be murdered, and myriads more dragged into the basest slavery.[10]

Likewise, Catholic missionary and anthropologist Bartolomé de Las Casas took his stand against European colonialism, many of whose practices he considered evil.[11]

One could argue that the very names of the slave ships on which Africans came to the land of the free belies the claim of ignorance. Those ships bore names such as *Brotherhood, Justice, Integrity, Gift of God,* and *Liberty.* There was even a ship named *Jesus.*[12] Assigning such spiritual names to slave ships seems to constitute a classic attempt at rationalization, in this case, trying to justify the Christian morality of the slave trade. Some then and now would view the naming of the slave ships as thinly veiled attempts to run from the reality of the evil that was being perpetrated.

Attempts to be more candid about the dark side of American history have been met with resistance by conservatives who want to emphasize only the good. On one of his radio shows, James Dobson led the charge against Goals 2000 and its National History Standards Project. We agree with some of his critique. The history standards do appear to be biased in favor of the political Left. But nowhere does he acknowledge the possibility that some of the efforts of revisionists represent healthy correctives. Instead, one of the guests on his show criticizes the proposed history standards because they advance "the notion that America is just one country among many" with "no recognition of America as the most wonderful place God has ever created on earth as a country."[13]

As moderates, we believe that some correctives are long overdue. For generations, American young people have learned in school about the bravery of the founding fathers. We learned about Paul Revere's ride; some of us even learned the name of his horse. We learned that George Washington was so honest he admitted to chopping down a cherry tree and that Abe Lincoln walked miles to return a woman's penny.

Do our children know about the millions of Native Americans who died while the United States became the greatest nation on earth? They know that the Indians scalped the white men, but do they know anything abut North American culture prior to the arrival of Europeans? Can they imagine the stench of death and human waste below the deck of a slave ship in the same way they can imagine those soldiers' cold feet at Valley Forge? Have they had the opportunity to reconsider the purity of the Puritans, some of whom cited passages from the Old Testament to justify the murder of women and children in the name of God? Puritan William Pynchon maintained that God fought for the white settlers "because He demanded . . . the complete submission of the natives to the true faith. When the [Pequot Indians] refused to submit . . . they signed their own death warrant."[14]

A Word to the Right

At the heart of the debate over school textbooks is a philosophical issue that remains unresolved. Some contend that the role of the educational system is not just to represent all sides, but to produce patriotic citizens. That being the case, they maintain that the "truth" should be presented within a context of support for the nation and its goals. This, of course, makes it something other than truth.

This same dilemma confronts journalists during wartime. Should they be committed to the truth no matter the cost, or should their commitment to the truth submit to national loyalty? According to most Christian conservatives, we are at war, albeit a cultural war. That being the case, perhaps they believe that managing truth is in the best interests of the nation.

As moderates, we maintain that the educational system can do both: develop patriotic citizens *and* tell the truth. We see nothing wrong with young children learning about their country in ways that engender love for their nation. But as they grow older, they need to be exposed to facts that challenge the view of America's purity. This is only fair to Native Americans and African-Americans, who, after all, are Americans, too.

We wonder about the extent to which conservatives can tolerate a balanced examination of history, one that tells the true story of America, warts and all. Are we secure enough as a nation to acknowledge the dark chapters of our past? Or will we dismiss honest critiques simply as concessions to what is "politically correct"?

We reject Rush Limbaugh's view that nothing that happened 250 years ago matters because that was then and this is now. The whole point of studying history is to learn who we are today based on who we used to be. De Tocqueville, who had mostly wonderful things to say about the American experiment when he visited the United States in the 1830s, did notice our proclivity for violence. (Based on statistics related to violent crime, he would probably make the same observation if he were with us today.) To explore our culture's historical propensity to violence—and to ask how it might be finding expression today—should not be deemed unpatriotic.

Many religious conservatives argue that America was founded as a "Christian nation" and that we need to make it a Christian nation again. The view of the United States as a Christian nation contributed to the concept of Manifest Destiny, according to which this country was established by God to fulfill a unique mission in the world. Such a view conforms to what Loren Mead calls the Christendom paradigm, in which the role of the church in previous generations was very closely identified with the role of

America. Mission took on an imperialistic flavor. Spreading western cultural values became synonymous in the minds of many with Christian mission. Even today, many people in a sense consider a Buddhist or an atheist un-American, since Americans are, virtually by definition, Christians.

The view of America's cultural superiority is evident in such bumper sticker messages as "America: Love It or Leave It" and "America Right or Wrong." At the Christian Coalition's 1995 conference, Pat Robertson was one of several speakers who assumed that, for all practical purposes, America is God's chosen nation. Such an attitude leads to a crusade mentality that assumes the moral superiority of America. According to this mentality, if America goes to war, that war must be just. If Christians in other lands die as a result of American bombs and bullets, so be it. They must be sacrificed for the larger cause of Christian values.

As moderates, we categorically reject the notion that God is working through this nation in ways he is not working through Christians in other lands. The biblical evidence strongly points toward the church, as opposed to any individual nation, as being the new Israel. Christians from the United States in general would be hard-pressed to develop a theology of nationalism according to which they owe greater loyalty to their own country than to brothers and sisters who hail from other nations.

To take healthy pride in one's place of origin is one thing. But for Christians to support their nation uncritically and unconditionally amounts, in our opinion, to idolatry. The role of the church is to stand outside the nation in an effort to evaluate it based on scriptural principles. A "love it or leave it" mentality is both un-American and un-Christian. A person does not exemplify love for America by turning a blind eye to its shortcomings. Christians from the United States would do well to take a short pilgrimage to Haiti, the poorest country in the Western Hemisphere, and to listen closely to what American missionaries there say about their own country's contributions to Haiti's dehumanizing poverty. If a conservative is a liberal who's been mugged, a liberal is a conservative who's been to Haiti.

According to biographer Gerald McDermott, Jonathan Edwards "commended patriotism as a natural and loving response to the needs of one's nation."[15] But he also "warned that patriotism often serves as a mask for self-interest." According to McDermott, Edwards would be wary "of contemporary calls to regard America as a Christian nation needing to return to its lost Christian roots." Instead, Edwards insisted that "no nation has ever been Christian." McDermott adds, "Edwards condemned eighteenth century New England for its religious hypocrisy, social strife, lack of compassion for the poor, and exploitation of Native Americans."

Likewise, we must question policies that appear to be based solely on national interest. Orthodox Christian doctrine clearly implies that national selfishness is no more justified than individual selfishness. As Reinhold Niebuhr pointed out in *Moral Man and Immoral Society*, the selfishness and exaggerated self-esteem in individuals are much more pronounced in nations. After all, individuals are sometimes moved by compassion or sympathy to sacrifice their own self-interests, whereas nations, as corporate entities, pursue their interests unswervingly. Even humanitarian aid is typically distributed with political considerations in mind.

To be sure, nations will behave selfishly as long as nations exist. But to acquiesce in the selfishness of one's nation is to conform to the way of the world and to abandon *agape*.

Advocating the application of religiously based moral principles in the international arena is not wrong. Given the instinctive American tendency to identify cultural and Christian values, however, it is incumbent on evangelicals to distinguish between the two. Among the most shameful chapters of Christian history are those in which people of faith uncritically—sometimes even fanatically—endorsed the ambition and moral arrogance of their national governments at the expense of biblical values.

A Word to the Left

Nevertheless, to believe that a nation's goals should be the same as the goals of the human race, seems naïve and simplistic.

Some politically radical idealists on the Left want to abolish nations so that all people might become merely citizens of the world. While we should be wary of nationalism, the Bible cannot be interpreted as unconditionally opposing the formation of nations. The admonition for Christians to love all people is perfectly consistent with the formation of bonds with people and places, based on political, cultural, and religious values.

The church should serve the country by evaluating policies in the light of biblical principles. Judging America, however, must come to mean more than finding fault with it. Perhaps Ronald Reagan went too far in calling the Soviet Union the "focus of evil in the world." But according to some on the Left, the United States deserves that designation. During the Cold War, Christians on the political Left, as represented by the National Council of Churches and in such publications as *Sojourners*, tended to treat the United States and the U.S.S.R. as moral equivalents. They defended such an approach by citing their responsibility to worry about their own country, and not about others.

To be a fair judge, however, one must be willing to call attention to the positive as well as the negative. At the very least, America's Christian critics during the Cold War should have been more specific regarding the standards by which they were comparing the two superpowers. That would have forced the acknowledgement of the fact that, with regard to political and religious freedom, simply no comparison existed.

Apparently, some on the Left fail to appreciate the incredible visionary nature of such principles as human dignity and individual religious and political freedom. These ideas were rooted solidly in an earlier, theological revolution, namely, the Reformation, which advanced the radical, liberating idea that individuals could approach God directly. The Left would do well to recall that Martin Luther King, Jr., in his critique of America, did not say that it was fundamentally flawed, but that it had failed to live up to its founding principles. Of course, the implication is that those founding principles were honorable and remain so.

Despite America's faults, people from all over the world are still eager to get here. Many are willing to risk their lives and to leave everything behind just to get here. They seek the same ideals of political and economic freedom that many Americans take for granted. We must recognize that at least some of this country's social and economic problems are rooted in its magnanimity, exemplified by its willingness through the years to open its doors to "huddled masses yearning to breathe free."

After all is said and done, a person cannot go to China and become Chinese or to Haiti and become a Haitian. But people can come from anywhere to the United States and become Americans. The concept of "Americanism," which is not based primarily on ethnic or linguistic considerations, is unique to this nation. There is no such thing as "Britishism" or "Germanism." And, over two centuries later, "Americanism" still connotes to many around the globe the very best of what the founding fathers had in mind. The worldwide movement for human rights could not have originated in China or many other nations around the world.

In conclusion, we believe that on balance, the American experiment has succeeded in making an unprecedented contribution to civilization. We believe this contribution is consistent with scriptural principles related to human dignity and justice. But as moderates, we also maintain that assessing the claim that America is the greatest nation on earth is an exercise in futility that is ultimately unhelpful in shaping the Christian mission. If conservatives come close to idolatry, and liberals border on smug cynicism, moderates must find their own place on the continuum that lies between such extremes. In evaluating this nation's history and purposes, as well as its behavior today, we must accept the responsibility to criticize when appropriate while giving credit when credit is due.

POINTS OF UNITY

All Christians should be able to agree that the United States is capable of doing both good and evil. America does not stand outside the judgment of God or the church. We should affirm the essentially biblical value of political freedom, while acknowledging that this freedom has led to immoral choices. Some Americans continue to pay the price for those immoral choices. Regardless of political beliefs, we should be sure at least to hear and consider the perspectives of those who have been injured.

Chapter Seven

Church Versus State

It's against my religion to impose my religion on others.

U.S. Senator John Ashcroft of Missouri at the
Christian Coalition's 1995 Road to Victory conference

The church-state debate has become one of the most common arenas in which conservatives and liberals battle one another. When Thomas Jefferson wrote his 1802 letter to the Danbury (Conn.) Baptist Association, he undoubtedly had no idea that nearly two centuries later his metaphor of a "wall of separation" between church and state would be at the heart of such heated debate.

Some on the Left have attempted to use this phrase to argue that religion should have no connection whatsoever to public life. Those on the Right maintain that Jefferson's phrase has been misunderstood. As Ralph Reed puts it, "Relying entirely on this single passage from a cursory letter paints an incomplete (and wholly inaccurate) picture of Jefferson's views."[1] Among other things, Reed cites Jefferson's signing of a treaty in 1803 that included the provision of government funds to support the Kaskaskia Indian tribe's Roman Catholic Church and priest.

As is the case with contemporary American citizens, those who founded this nation were not in agreement on the question of the proper relationship between the institutions of religion and government. For some, the presumption that people with different religious beliefs could coexist was both radical and unworkable. That helps explain why the state of Maryland was founded for the purpose of providing a place for Catholics.

Divisions did not run strictly along secular versus religious lines. Christians themselves were of separate minds on the church-state question. The old jibe against Puritans is essentially true: "They loved religious liberty so much that they desired to keep it all for themselves." That is to say, the Puritans saw little if any distinction between church and state. In essence they advocated theocracy. In contrast, Baptist believers recognized distinct roles for both the church and the government. They maintained that the two institutions should steer clear from one another as much as possible.

The founders of this nation were wise enough to recognize the church-state tensions that would likely exist in a democracy. Their wisdom was enhanced by their awareness of the problems that state religion had caused in the Old World. On the one hand, they understood that the success of the American experiment was largely contingent on values, and they knew that values were inextricably tied to religion. Thus, they neither suppressed nor denied the important role of religious belief in forming the new society. But they also recognized the diversity of religious belief that surrounded them. Based on that recognition, they were committed to principles that would allow all people to practice the religion of their choice. These principles, of course, found expression in the First Amendment: "Congress shall make no law respecting the establishment of religion, or prohibiting the free exercise thereof." This was their way of saying that government should be neutral with respect to religion, that it should neither promote religion nor suppress it.

At the heart of the contemporary church-state debate are the following questions: Did our nation's founders intend to remain neutral only with respect to showing no favor to one religion over all others? Or did they intend to remain neutral with respect to religion in general? Conservatives tend to argue the former. Thus,

Ralph Reed and others affirm the concept of "civil religion," according to which government-sponsored support of generic religious values is acceptable so long as those values are not linked to a particular set of religious beliefs.

Much of the contemporary church-state debate addresses the question of what the founding fathers truly intended. When Norman Lear set out to oppose the Moral Majority, he named his organization "People for the American Way" (PAW). Along with the American Civil Liberties Union (ACLU) and Americans United for the Separation of Church and State, PAW believes that if the founding fathers could speak to us today, they would, based on their tolerance for people of no religious faith, oppose government-sponsored religious expression in any form.

Organizations on the Left and on the Right both claim to represent the true "American way." Further, they claim that those on the other side pose a threat to this country's most cherished values. As in the previous chapter, we call attention to James Skillen's assessment of the "long-held but increasingly murky myth of America's moral/cultural unity."[2] In other words, perhaps we are not united today because we never really ever were.

If this is the case, we may be no closer today to resolving the church-state debate than our forefathers were 200 years ago. Now, as then, we recognize the relationships that exist between religious faith and values and between values and the success of the nation. But, although faith is good for the nation, we cannot simply require people to accept faith. That would violate the value of religious freedom. The recognition that faith contributes to values stands in tension with the principle that faith cannot be legislated. Our task as citizens—and as a society—is to determine how these worthy values can coexist.

A MODERATE PERSPECTIVE

Christians engaged in the church-state debate have spent too much time arguing over what Jefferson had to say about the separation of church and state and not enough time examining what the Bible teaches. Jesus said, "Give to Caesar what is Caesar's, and to God what is God's" (Matt. 22:21). This suggests his recognition of church and state as distinct institutions. Taking issue with those who advocate theocracy, we contend that the Bible treats the kingdom of God as a spiritual and not a political reality.

We affirm the principle of religious freedom as a firmly grounded scriptural concept. God calls people to faith individually, not through government. God allows human beings the freedom to choose to follow him or to reject him.

A majority of the people who broke from Great Britain to found America were Christians. And even those who were not were influenced by the moral precepts of the Bible. Yet the Constitution explicitly rejects the idea that religious belief should be legislated. There can be no doubt that this nation was not founded as a "Christian nation" in the theocratic sense. The Constitution plainly rejects theocracy.

Undoubtedly it was difficult to uphold the principle of religious freedom in a nation where many held strong Christian beliefs. Historian Mark Noll writes that

> leaders like James Madison realized that the question of religion was explosive and complicated. Any effort to establish one particular faith would have drawn violent protests from adherents of other denominations. Yet any effort to deny the importance of religion would have deeply offended the substantial numbers who still believed that the health of a nation depended upon the health of its faith.[3]

According to Noll, the "compromise chosen by the founding fathers was to avoid the issue," in essence by relegating these issues to the states.[4]

This resulted in Christianity enjoying privileged status. Noll points out that in 1791, when the First Amendment was put into practice, five of the nation's 14 states supported ministers through taxes. Writes Noll, "Only Virginia and Rhode Island enjoyed the sort of 'separation of church and state' that Americans now take for granted, that is, where government provides no tax money for churches and poses no religious conditions for participation in public life."[5]

Favoritism of the Christian religion continued in various forms for decades in apparent violation of the principles established by the Constitution. For example, it was favored through government-sponsored prayer in public schools. Conservatives typically cite the Supreme Court's 1962 decision to ban school prayer as the turning point in America's moral decline. But this decision, while bucking tradition, was perfectly consistent with the principles of the Constitution. As political scientist John Vile writes, the decision was not "predicated on opposition to religion," but was "based on a legitimate concern for the rights of non-Christians in an increasingly pluralistic society."[6] The High Court in 1962, we must remember, did not ban prayer in public schools. It banned only *government sponsored and initiated* prayer.

In recent decades, the evangelical community in general has come to a greater appreciation of the importance of religious freedom as a constitutional principle. Many have realized that if this principle is not preserved, the kinds of laws enacted in the past to advance Christianity at the expense of other religions could—in a different cultural climate—be used to oppress the Christian faith. Thus, virtually all Christian legal organizations joined with civil liberties groups, including the ACLU, to oppose the Supreme Court's 1990 decision not to allow Native Americans to smoke peyote as a religious rite. Even though evangelicals do not personally endorse the use of peyote, they recognized that if suppression of religion is accepted in theory, it could at some point be applied to them.

In evaluating the effect of the current Supreme Court on religion, we should consider the perspective of Christian Legal Society attorney Steve McFarland: "One of the pivotal mistaken assumptions that the Religious Right has made is the assumption that any nominee for the U.S. Supreme Court proposed by a conservative Republican President is good for America or at least good for the Religious Right's agenda." McFarland maintains that the "staunchest defenders of the free exercise clause" of the First Amendment are the "liberals" on the court.[7]

"Majoritarianism" or "Tyranny of the Minority"?

Our affirmation of the principle of religious freedom means that we must take issue with a statement made by Congressman John Kasich of Ohio at the Christian Coalition's 1995 Road to Victory conference. Kasich said that to allow one student who does not want to pray to get his way at the expense of the 99 who want to pray constitutes "tyranny of the minority."

For one thing, Kasich's argument presents practical problems. What if only 97 want to pray and 3 don't? What about a margin of 67 to 33? Or 51 to 49? More importantly, the flip side of Kasich's concern about the tyranny of the minority is the concern about "majoritarianism," or requiring the submission of all to the will of the majority.

The genius of the American experiment is not that the majority rules in all situations but that the freedoms of the minority are honored wherever possible. There are, no doubt, some church-state conflicts where tough decisions must be made regarding whose rights should be given priority. But in many instances, creative solutions can be found to honor the principles that both sides are trying to protect. Unfortunately, ideologues are too busy shouting at each other and insisting on their own "solutions" to explore all the possibilities.

Since it began in 1984, the National Association for Released Time Christian Education has employed a creative solution to the church-state debate in public schools.[8] Each week public school students may leave their schools for a time to receive religious education at the place of their choice. This affirms religious freedom while also affirming a connection between religion and morality.

There is no reason why this concept could not be applied everywhere in the United States. Christian young people would go to their churches, Jewish children to the temple, Muslims to the mosques. Atheists and agnostics would also be free to go to places of their own choosing.

The Myth of Neutrality

Unfortunately, organizations on the political Left, the ACLU being chief among them, maintain that the only way to preserve religious freedom is to suppress public expression of religious faith. The argument that the public square must remain neutral with respect to religion presumes incorrectly that the absence of religion constitutes neutrality. In its 1963 *Abingdon v. Schempp* decision, the Supreme Court declared that reading the Bible as a devotional exercise in public schools is unconstitutional. But the majority opinion made it clear that this decision was not based on opposition to religion and was not intended to create "a religion of secularism."

This decision implicitly recognizes that neutrality with respect to religion does not exist. All people bring to the public debate a worldview and its corresponding values. Why should a nonreligious worldview be considered any more legitimate than a religious one? The answer is, it shouldn't. In 1995 President Clinton affirmed that "the First Amendment does not convert our schools into religion-free zones."[9]

Denying Christians or Muslims or Buddhists the right to express their religious faith in the public square does not constitute neutrality; it merely stacks the deck against religious people. The goal should not be to eliminate expressions of religious faith, but to grant all people equal rights to express their faith and to protect all people from being forced to participate in exercises of faith against their will.

If we are to move beyond the stalemate that divides the political Left and Right, the ACLU and other groups with similar public policy agendas will simply have to acknowledge the validity of bringing a religious perspective to the public policy debate. Every citizen has the right to support or oppose public policies based on one's personal values as a Christian, a Hindu, a Buddhist, an atheist, or a secular humanist.

We agree in principle with the message of the bumper sticker "Religion in our lives, not in our laws." But while we oppose religion in our laws, we dare not oppose values in our laws. And for most Americans, the basis for those values is still religion.

The relationship between a society's religious values and its laws is undeniable. Laws are not negated because the values they espouse happen to coincide with religious teachings. No one in his or her right mind would argue that laws prohibiting murder, rape, or stealing are invalid because they favor Christianity. Most laws are inherently moral. And so it stands to reason that the laws a society makes to govern itself will be rooted in the morality of the citizenry.

Laws, based on moral principles, effectively limit the freedoms of some people in order to guard the lives, health, or freedom of other people. For example, through legislation and organizational policies, this country has limited in recent years the freedom of smokers to protect the right of nonsmokers to be healthy. By confining smoking to designated areas, we have sought a moderate solution to a problem.

If we had the political will, we could outlaw smoking altogether. In fact, we the people can do anything we want to do if we can simply persuade enough people. That's how our democracy works. Christians have the right to vote for candidates who promise to restore government-sponsored prayer to public schools. They even have the right to vote for people who want to create a theocracy in America. While we would not oppose that objective on constitutional grounds, we would on biblical and moral grounds.

The Guiding Principle

Christians who are active in the public debate can and must bring their Bible-based values to bear. But among those values must be a respect for the religious freedom of all citizens. In order to balance this tension, we propose the following principle: Christians operating in the public square must distinguish between their advocacy of moral principles based on Christian faith and their advocacy of principles intended to promote the religion of Christianity. This recognizes a distinction between laws that represent the moral values of religious people and "religious laws" (laws that propagate religious belief).

We realize that the principle we propose will not resolve the debate among Christians. People will continue to disagree about whether a particular law or policy represents Christian values or if it promotes Christianity. Nevertheless, this principle enables us to make some distinctions. For example, it enables us to conclude that specifically Christian government- sponsored prayer in public schools violates the constitutional principle of religious freedom. Those who advocate such prayer are behaving as theocrats, whether they admit it or not.

The Christian Coalition's yearly conferences and other conservative gatherings routinely feature stories of how the Christian voice is suppressed in the public school context. These stories include that of a seven-year-old child who was humiliated by her teacher for the sin of addressing a valentine to Jesus. In another situation, Muslim students were allowed to pray, but Christians were not.

We suspect that some conservatives overstate the problem by portraying such situations as the norm, rather than the exception. After all, surveys have indicated that in some parts of the Bible Belt, a solid majority of public school teachers are Protestant Christians. Nevertheless, we ignore these stories of abuse at our own peril.

It is likely that some public school teachers and administrators have from time to time limited religious expression because they are uncertain about what the law allows. In this litigious society, they fear a lawsuit. Many believe the best way to avoid one is to promote a "religion-free" school environment.

The 1995 document "A Joint Statement of Current Law" was developed to address this very concern. Supported by dozens of organizations, including the National Association of Evangelicals, the Christian Legal Society, and the ACLU, this document affirms that, according to current law, students are allowed to pray in schools, are permitted to read their Bibles, and may express their religious faith in the classroom and in written assignments. Those who claim that the Supreme Court has abolished religious expression in public schools simply are not telling the truth.

Unfortunately, in some instances the Supreme Court has appeared uncertain about whether the rights of Christians to express themselves deserve equal protection. The case *Rosenberger v. Rector* addressed the question of whether Christian college students had the same access to school funds as other religious (or nonreligious) organizations. In this case, the High Court affirmed those rights, but the vote was only 5–4 and there are indications that some on the majority were voting based on the facts of this particular case, not on the principle of granting equal protection to Christians.[10]

Some people feel that it is acceptable to limit Christian expression because Christianity is this country's majority religion. In fact, the United States does have more churches per capita than any other country in the world. It is assumed, therefore, that Christianity faces no threat of extinction. Yet such an argument should count for nothing in light of the importance of protecting a fundamental constitutional right. Followers of Christ should be given the same freedoms of expression granted to people of other faiths and to people of no faith. If that principle is not guarded diligently, the legitimate rights of Christians to exert their influence in the public square are at risk of being unconstitutionally denied.

The Question of Civil Religion

Among Christians, the issue of civil religion lies at the heart of church-state questions. The civil religion debate focuses on whether government-endorsed expression of generic religious beliefs should be tolerated. This country's civil religion is expressed in various ways. For example, our coins still say "In God We Trust," the President's oath of office makes reference to God, and Congress begins its sessions with prayer. Those who support government-sponsored prayer and the posting of the Ten Commandments in public schools base their arguments on a high view of civil religion.

Most of us can agree on what civil religion is, but we do not agree on whether it is good for Christianity and for the country. Believing it is a good thing, Ralph Reed threads this theme throughout his book *Politically Incorrect*. For example, he chides the Supreme Court for finding unconstitutional an "innocuous prayer" by a Jewish rabbi at a graduation ceremony, claiming that the decision "rejected America's centuries-old tradition of civil religion. . . ."[11]

Loren Mead maintains that from the beginning, civil religion in the United States has been "a creature of custom, never of law" and that it has "led to a kind of cultural religion that pledges quasi-religious allegiance to flag and country." Evangelical moderate Tom Sine maintains that civil religion and Christianity are two "totally different faiths." He adds, "It is absolutely incomprehensible to me how a follower of Jesus Christ can worship at two very different altars and serve two very different Gods."[12]

As moderates, we oppose civil religion for a variety of reasons. For one thing, while it may feel comfortable to religious people, it ignores the rights of the nonreligious. More importantly, civil religion distorts Christian faith, which we hold to be true. As Christians, we take issue with Ralph Reed in that we feel there is no such thing as an "innocuous prayer."

At the Christian Coalition's 1995 Road to Victory conference, one of those in attendance made an interesting and telling remark during a workshop. He observed that after the Supreme Court banned school prayer, most schools in his home state of Mississippi went right on praying anyway. Then he said that those schools were facing exactly the same problems as other schools that had quit praying. This calls into question the analysis of Pat Robertson and others on the Right, namely, that this country's current problems began with bad Supreme Court decisions handed down in the '60s and '70s.

Many on the Right have allowed the Supreme Court's school prayer decision to become a scapegoat for what is wrong with

America. They think if we would only bring back prayer and the Ten Commandments, things would be well again. But that is naïve and misleading. Civil religion is ultimately an empty religion. It has done nothing for members of Congress who have lied, cheated, or abused women. It cannot change lives. Jesus Christ alone can do that.

POINTS OF UNITY

Christians ought to be able to affirm in principle both that the Constitution does not mandate religious belief and that neutrality in the public square is a myth. We should affirm a distinction between laws that represent Christian values and laws that promote religion, even if we cannot always agree on which is which. Finally, while we may be at odds over whether civil religion is a good option, we should proclaim that a relationship with Jesus Christ is a better one.

Chapter Eight

The Role of Government

Tragically, we have witnessed in Oklahoma City the logical derivative of the rhetoric of Rush Limbaugh and his ilk. Please, people, 'the government' isn't the enemy; the government is us. Attacking it attacks all of us. If it doesn't work, let's fix it.

Joe Morse in a letter to *Time*[1]

The church-state debate in America has a close cousin: the debate over the appropriate size and role of government. This debate spans issues related to economic systems, taxation, education, welfare, and more. Generally speaking, opponents line up behind the same ideological lines that divide them on church-state issues.

Conservatives affirm the maxim, "Government that governs least, governs best." They believe that federal government should be confined to national defense and coordinating the nation's infrastructures. In keeping with that view, conservatives favor lower taxes and, based on the belief that the free market knows best, are inclined to oppose government regulations.

Motivated largely by the goal to balance the federal budget, conservatives highlight the inefficiency of government in general and the current inefficiency of the welfare system in particular. In addition, many have called for the dissolution of the federal Department of Education in order to bring education back under the control of local communities and thus, they think, of parents.

Finding people at the opposite extreme—those who believe that government can solve all the nation's problems—is not as easy as it used to be. The era of the classic political liberal has ended. It ended in part because, not only did the United States lose a war in Vietnam in the '60s and '70s, but we also lost the "War on Poverty." Few dispute that the liberal policies of the last generation hurt many of the very people they were intended to help.

Not all of those who gave up on classic liberalism, however, moved all the way to Right. Instead, they carved out their ideological niche at a different place, a place still to the Left of the conservatives. Like their conservative counterparts, today's liberals want to eliminate the federal deficit, but they advocate different ways of doing it. For example, they would much rather cut defense spending than social programs.

In addition, today's liberals believe that government has a legitimate and important role to play in education and in the development and enforcement of regulations in such areas as the environment, health care, and the workplace. Though they may not like taxes any more than conservatives, they tolerate them more readily, especially when the tax structure demands more of the rich than the poor.

A MODERATE VIEWPOINT

As the letter introducing this chapter suggests, the 1994 Oklahoma City bombing reminded us that the government is ultimately not some impersonal, nameless, and faceless identity. It is people, people who go to church and shop in grocery stores with the rest of us. It is people with emotions, who will miss their children and their coworkers who were lost in this tragedy.

Many government "bureaucrats" are in fact faithful, hard-working, decent people who have made significant contributions to their communities and to this country through government service. Some of these people no doubt feel trapped in bad systems and are as frustrated as everyone else.

It is unfair to conclude that the conservative talk show hosts were responsible for the Oklahoma City bombing, but certainly their rhetoric did not help. As Congressman Charles Stenholm puts it, "Polarization driven by individual interest and enforced by a ceaseless negativism about our government is extremely unhealthy for the country."[2]

Government is not, as the rhetoric of some conservatives would have us conclude, an unmitigated evil. The Bible treats government as a necessity. In Romans 13 Paul writes that government, even the pagan government of the Roman Empire, is neither demonic nor contrary to the ordinances of God. Jesus reflects the view that God ordains government when he tells Pilate, "You would have no power over me if it were not given to you from above" (John 19:11).

The fact that government is ordained by God does not shelter it from the criticism of the people it is supposed to represent. But it is incumbent upon those citizens to acknowledge both the good and the bad. Many government programs through the years have enriched individual Americans and the country in general. For example, most would consider the G.I. Bill, which gave hundreds of thousands of deserving military veterans a chance for an education, to be an unmitigated success. Few today would criticize the federal government's positive influence on civil rights legislation in the '60s and '70s. Head Start and hot lunch programs have given countless young people a chance they might not otherwise have had. Despite its problems, the public school system has succeeded and continues to succeed for millions of American youth. Even welfare has worked the way it was intended to work for countless Americans, including one of the authors.

As conservatives contend, it is certainly true that the very nature—and size—of government renders it incapable of performing some tasks efficiently. Conservatives believe that government's "efficiency quotient" will increase with the transfer of authority from the federal to state and local levels. Such a contention is clearly open to debate.

We must realize that, historically, some responsibilities have been turned over to the federal government because local governments were not in the best political position to do what needed to be done. Civil rights legislation is a good example. We suspect that most Americans, even if they deny the reality of contemporary racism, concede that this was a racist nation prior to the civil rights movement. Had these highly moral reforms been left to local governments, resistance in communities throughout the nation would have guaranteed failure in many locales. People knew where their local county or city council representatives lived and could pursue them directly. The federal government maintains its distance.

Conservatives are generally concerned about the size of government, especially the federal government. As moderates, we believe the primary criterion for evaluating government is not size, but quality. We should ask the following of specific policies and philosophies: Is this good or bad government? Is this appropriate or inappropriate government?

A document drafted by the Washington, D.C.-based Center for Public Justice (CPJ) is most helpful on this score.[3] Though it focuses on welfare reform, the critique it offers applies to all aspects of government. The essay explores this country's "responsibility crisis" wherein government has been allowed to assume too much responsibility at the expense of other social and cultural entities, including families, schools, and private citizens. But the answer, the essay suggests, does not lie in the wholesale abandonment of government, but in refocusing government's role in ways that support, rather than inhibit, other institutions in society.

In this regard, we acknowledge the legitimacy of the Right's concern that the rights of parents, families, and other social institutions are sometimes wrongly suppressed because government has overstepped its bounds. For example, many public school administrators through their policies and attitudes seem to assume that they "own" our children instead of viewing their role as that of servants.

In Romans 13 Paul addresses the issue of government and servanthood. And his views fly in the face of the self-image of the Roman Empire. For example, he criticizes its legal structure and downgrades its claims to authority. He makes it clear that, while governments are ordained by God, they do not exist for themselves. Their purpose is to serve for good, not to dominate. According to Paul, government should receive what it is due, but nothing more.

While not the only factor, the size of government is a key indication of how government views itself in terms of its servanthood role. Congressman Dick Armey of Texas points out that in 1948 the average family paid 2 percent in taxes and that today it pays 24 percent. He states, "Millions of families today need a second earner not to support the family but to support the government."[4] Ralph Reed points out that when the Department of Agriculture began in 1862, it employed just 9 people even though 60 percent of Americans worked on farms. Today, with only 3 percent of Americans working on farms, that department employees 150,000. Pat Robertson points out that the middle class spends more on taxes than on household expenses.[5]

We believe that the size of government today suggests that it has to some extent lost sight of the proper roles of other social and cultural institutions. According to the classic illustration, the best way to kill a fly is with a fly swatter. Using a cannon will get the job done, but it will create other problems. When government loses sight of its limitations, it can create more problems than it solves.

Let us remember, though, that government got too big because we allowed it to happen. As William Bennett observes, "It wasn't just a power grab. Some people didn't want to take responsibility."[6] In other words, government at times in the past acted when others could not—or would not—take the initiative. Historical examples include the Great Depression, the civil rights movement, and, we contend, concern for the environment. This is not to say that the government's response was always good, but it acted out of necessity.

Some of what we have given to government we can and should take back. From all appearances, however, as a culture we are confused and uncertain, and far from consensus with regard to the proper delegation of rights and responsibilities. Some people have attempted to exploit that confusion. Instead of working to develop a sound, consistent philosophy of limited government, politicos on both sides of the aisle tend toward wanting to use government authority as a hammer to accomplish their broader political and social agendas. CPJ President James Skillen makes this observation in his critique of the Christian Coalition's Contract with the American Family. Skillen observes that the Contract's

> alternate attacks on and appeals to the federal government do not emerge from a clear principle of discrimination but are determined by their usefulness to the coalition's civil-religious mobilizing aims. Where the broad public, to which the coalition appeals, appears sympathetic to a national anti-pornography crusade, the coalition is willing to go straight to the federal government to ask it to do what the coalition believes is the right and moral thing to do. On the other hand, where the coalition senses that 'the American people' feel antagonism toward the federal government, it is not hesitant to speak as if the federal government is the enemy of families, schools, charities, and people generally.[7]

What we need is a consistent philosophy of limited federal government, one that allows churches, businesses, individuals, families, and government to do what each institution does best. For example, government programs should emphasize investment as opposed to consumption, should benefit diverse constituencies as opposed to special interest lobbies, should provide services that the market cannot or is not providing, and in most cases should not give without requiring something in return. And when in doubt, we should do without.

Economic Systems

The Bible supplies us with principles by which to evaluate economic systems, but it does not unequivocally recommend any one system over all others. Writes Tom Sine, "Frankly, the reason I believe free enterprise works so well is that its chief motive force is the naked self-interest of fallen human beings."[8] Such sentiment, we believe, is only a partial explanation for capitalism's success. In fact, capitalism is based in part on the highly moral notion of providing goods and services that meet the needs and wants of human beings. It is difficult to dispute the contention that a free, decentralized market is more efficient and thus, many would contend, more moral than the alternatives. What's more, the idea of economic freedom follows naturally from the concept of political freedom.

Yet we recognize that capitalism is not monolithic. In its purest form, it upholds Lockean traditions of respect for individuals and for the integrity of local communities. At its best, it considers not just the current year's bottom line, but the long-range interests of individuals, communities, and the society at large. This presupposes a responsibility to future generations, as demonstrated through concern for environmental care.

Criticizing capitalism is not as fashionable today as it was a decade or so ago. We are still basking in the glow of our Cold War victory over another economic system that went bankrupt. Nevertheless, we agree with whoever said, "The problem with socialism is socialism. The problem with capitalism is capitalists."

Adam Smith would likely cringe today if he could witness some of what is being done by his economic ancestors in the name of capitalism. When a concern for the "bottom line" dominates respect for individuals and violates fundamental principles of fairness, this is morally wrong whether it happens within a capitalistic or socialistic economic system.

Capitalism functions as it should when it functions in a context of commitment to moral principles. It must be contained when moral principles are ignored to the extent that powerless human beings are placed at risk. This was the basis for child labor laws, whose legitimacy only the most radical of conservatives contest.

When the free market loses sight of fundamental principles of human dignity and fairness, it must be restrained. Fiscally healthy U.S. companies who offer low wages and no benefits to desperate men and women along the Mexican border are not practicing capitalism; they are exploiting human beings.

The same can be said of companies who refuse to offer health benefits to their employees even when they are financially capable of doing so. As moderates, we recognize that for some small or mid-size businesses, generous employee benefits might be the fastest road to extinction. Therefore, we make a distinction between them and the financially capable companies who refuse to offer benefits only so the top executives can have three cars instead of two or can add a swimming pool to their backyards. We believe that a moral critique of the abuses of the market has been noticeably absent from the Right's analysis.

The Christian community is divided over the extent to which such concerns as those described above ought to be considered issues of "economic justice," and therefore open to correction by government, as over against private morality. Nevertheless, we affirm the rights of believers to advocate, through political means, economic policies that respect the humanity of individuals and that enhance the ideals of community.

For example, they might support some sort of proportional relationship between the remuneration offered to a company's highest paid and lowest paid employees. Granted, a policy according to which all employees are paid equally would destroy incentive and fail to recognize those who made the sacrifices necessary to move to a higher level. But what about a policy mandating that the highest paid employee could make no more than 20 to 40 times the amount of its lowest paid employee? The percentage could be adjusted based on years of service and level of responsibility. The incentive to make $800,000 instead of $20,000 would remain, but the policy would establish a relationship between the business's success and rewards for all its employees. This policy would place top executives in relationship with all employees and encourage them to treat those employees with dignity, as opposed to replacing cheap labor with cheap labor for the sake of the bottom line. (Such a policy would be great news for the employees of the Disney Company, whose top executive, Michael Eisner, makes over $200 million a year!)[9]

We the people have the right to authorize government to step in to protect citizens from the moral abuses of the free market. This includes the regulation of businesses. No one would deny that in some instances government regulations have gone too far and thus have become cumbersome and restraining. However, we wonder how many of those who oppose all government regulation would set foot on an airplane or eat at a restaurant that did not comply with the safety and health standards set by our federal government. Again, the focus of the debate should be on distinguishing between appropriate and inappropriate regulations.

Finally, as moderates, we believe that both private enterprise and government have the right and responsibility to address the needs of those who have been economically displaced. In Adam Smith's day, people could not enjoy prosperity without bringing plenty of others along with them. In the industrial age, when workers were in high demand, wealth was more likely to trickle down.

But times have changed. Jobs that people used to do are now being done by computers or other machines. We do not contend, as some do, that modern technology inevitably contributes to unemployment. According to James K. Glassman, the United States gained 35 million more jobs in 1994 than it lost.[10] We are suspicious of that figure, but regardless of its accuracy, no one can deny that technology has displaced some people. Industries that were thriving only a few decades ago have become obsolete. Steel towns have become ghost towns. People who went to school in the '50s and '60s to learn a trade have been rendered unmarketable. As a society, what will we say to the 55-year-old man who has lost his job, is willing to work, but has no marketable skills or talents? He's too young to go on a fixed income and too old to start over again. We maintain that it is perfectly appropriate for government to step in and address this problem, preferably in cooperation with private enterprise.

Public Education

Public education in the United States is far from a wasteland. This is not to say it has no problems, both in terms of its quality and the values it sometimes represents. As mentioned earlier, we believe that public education, as with government in general, has lost sight of its role as a servant and has assumed the role of dominance. As Ralph Reed puts it, "Although schools perform an important function, children ultimately belong to their parents, not the government."[11]

If public schools believed that, more of them would be willing to work with home schoolers instead of regarding them as enemies. Since parents of home-schooled children pay to support public education, they should have the opportunity to make use of public schools to the extent they desire. For example, home schoolers should not be prevented from taking a typing class or competing on the sports team of their local public school.

Public education's heightened notion of its authority took place gradually over the past several decades, but did not become an issue until the values it represented began to clash with the values of Americans, particularly conservative Christians. For example, James Dobson supports public education in theory, but is concerned when the values it espouses clash with the values of the people it is supposed to be serving. We maintain that public education can and should find ways to allow people of various religious faiths or of no religious faith to find expression in a context of equal opportunity.

With that said, however, let us not ignore the positive contributions public schools have made in the area of values. One of the authors' daughters came home one day from her public school and discussed her school project in relation to Martin Luther King Day. Even as a second-grader, she was able to articulate the contribution King, motivated by his Christian faith, made in advocating equal rights for all human beings through peaceful means. One cannot help but wonder how many conservative Christian schools throughout this land place a similar emphasis on the contributions of Martin Luther King, Jr.

Much of the debate over public education has focused on the issue of educational vouchers. We maintain that the public policy that guarantees all children the opportunity for an education is sound. Not only is an educated electorate necessary in a democracy, but Christians can justify support for public education in terms of a responsibility for the general welfare of the community. On the other hand, we recognize the priority of parental choice in education. We hear the pleas of those who are not availing themselves of the public education system but are required to pay for it anyway.

Those on one side of the voucher debate insist that it's all about making rich people richer. Those on the other side say it's about giving poor people a chance at a better educational opportunity for their children. Why can't we admit that, depending on the situation, both assessments are correct?

We propose a compromise. Parents of private-school children who can afford to send their children to private school without the help of vouchers should not receive vouchers. Based on a responsibility to the community, they should be required to help support public education, as are people who don't even have children. Those who could not afford to send their children to private schools without vouchers should be entitled to receive them, if that is what they want for their children. Those who are somewhere between rich and poor might be entitled to limited aid in the form of vouchers, based on family income. Such a plan would nullify the argument that vouchers are for the rich.

As with all of the issue-related chapters in this book, we have no delusions that the ideas and suggestions presented here are flawless or that the proposals are workable. We are merely attempting to set a tone and to encourage creative thinking and sound discussion.

POINTS OF UNITY

All Christians should be able to affirm that government is not by definition evil, that in fact it is ordained by God. Yet its purpose is not to control our lives, but to complement and support all of society's social and cultural institutions, including the family. We must never forget that government consists of people, and that people make government what it is.

Chapter Nine

Welfare

Let us be careful that we don't get caught up in the political
rhetoric that says, "Get tough." Let us never forget that one of
the reasons we are having to talk about getting tough is because
as Christian believers, we were the ones who failed to get tender
when it really counted in the lives of people.

Lieutenant Governor Mike Huckabee of Arkansas at the
Christian Coalition's 1995 Road to Victory conference

Even though Medicaid is a bigger drain on the federal budget,
the welfare system has for many come to symbolize all that is
wrong with government. The welfare system was intended to provide short-term, remedial aid for people facing temporary hard-
ship. It has evolved into a seemingly inefficient bureaucracy that,
many argue, is unintentionally hurting many of those it is supposed to be helping. In addition, some people, no doubt, have
intentionally misused the system.

To make matters worse, some welfare regulations provide
financial incentives for behavior that contradicts the values shared
by a majority of Americans. Chief among these values is the value
of intact families living together under one roof.

Welfare reform has become a rallying cry for both major
political parties. Democrats and Republicans have had no trouble
agreeing that something has to change. They disagree on some of

the details of that change, including the swiftness with which it ought to take place.

A MODERATE PERSPECTIVE

In his book *The Tragedy of American Compassion,* Marvin Olasky recounts a story that first appeared in the *Wall Street Journal* about a welfare mother who was determined to make the best of her meager monthly income.[1] Instead of buying new clothes, she bought used ones or made clothes for her daughter. Instead of purchasing toys at Toys 'R Us, she shopped at Goodwill. By being frugal and industrious, she was able to save $3,000 over four years. The government rewarded her by taking her to court, since according to the rules, she was not allowed to save more than $1,000.

This is just one story illustrating the need for welfare reform. There are many more. No one denies that the lessons welfare is teaching people are not the lessons they should be learning. Welfare regulations that offer incentives for families to live apart instead of together are morally wrong. Policies that encourage dependence, rather than personal initiative, are misguided. The system should function solely for the purpose of enabling people to work toward self-sufficiency, not just for the sake of the society but for their own sake as individuals.

Statistics cited by Merrill Matthews, Jr., health policy director for the National Center for Policy Analysis, document the system's inefficiency. According to Matthews, if the money designated for welfare were distributed to those living below the poverty line, a family of four would receive nearly $36,000 a year on which to live.[2]

We agree with many of the concerns raised by the Right about welfare. Yet evidence suggests that the welfare system has been made into something of a scapegoat for other societal ills, including crime, drugs, and illiteracy in the African-American community. According to Paul Offner, legislative assistant to U.S. Senator Daniel Patrick Moynihan of New York, black welfare dependency has declined from over 37 percent in 1973 to under 33 percent in 1993. During that same period, the above-mentioned problems worsened, rather than improved.[3]

Corporate Welfare

In addressing inefficiency and dishonesty in the distribution of government aid, policy makers should not limit the discussion to the poor. Middle class and wealthy people have exploited the system as well. It is common for someone who wants to leave his or her job to persuade the boss to structure the termination as a layoff so that unemployment benefits can be harvested. We suspect that most readers of this book know more people who fit that category than they know people on welfare.

Conservative Republicans have wanted to cut spending in every area of government except defense. Taxpayers' hard earned dollars are being used to keep big business up and running as usual, even though this runs counter to the expressed views of most Americans. In the absence of an impending military crisis, sparing defense the budget ax smacks of corporate welfare.

Ray Bakke asks, "Can we be honest and admit Boeing is on welfare, American farmers are on price supports, and the Acme Post Office and all rural post offices are not sustainable by 32 cent stamps?"[4] His point is that government subsidizes many groups, not just the poor.

In June 1995 the *Philadelphia Inquirer* ran a seven-part series on "high-tech handouts." Since 1975 the government has spent over $76 million on the Energy-Related Inventions Program (ERIP), which over the last two decades has provided grants to individuals and small corporations who have claimed to be able to develop a promising new technology. Over half of the money has been spent in overhead. As of 1992, only 668 people were employed by companies related to ERIP.[5]

In 1994 Citicorp, a bank with $250 billion in assets and $3.4 billion in profits, received $9.6 million in federal assistance in evaluating credit-risk problems. According to the *Philadelphia*

Inquirer, it is one of 1000 companies that are "receiving federal research help to develop technologies, solve manufacturing problems or sell new products."[6] Between 1990 and 1994, the federal government distributed millions of dollars in technology subsidies. Nearly $300 million of that went to eight corporations—Amoco, AT&T, Citicorp, DuPont, General Electric, General Motors, IBM, and Motorola—with a combined 1994 profit of $26 billion. According to the newspaper, "the return to taxpayers from licensing and royalty fees amounted to one-fifth of a penny on the dollar."[7]

The *Washington Post* reports that each year "the Defense Department inadvertently pays contractors hundreds of millions of dollars that it does not owe them, and much of the money is never returned. In addition, the department has spent $15 billion it cannot account for over the past decade."[8] Congressman John Kasich, the point man for addressing the budget deficit, was quoted in *Time* as saying, "There's so much waste and inefficiency in the operation of the Pentagon. We need to clean that up as much as we need to clean up any other department."[9] Fairness dictates that welfare programs for the poor should not receive discriminatory treatment.

A Compassionate Approach

Given the biblical mandate to care for the poor, Christians ought to focus on what constitutes genuine compassion. Decisions about welfare policies should be based not on what is good for taxpayers, but on what is best for the poor. Ultimately, policies that lead people to dependency are rooted not in compassion, but in ignorance.

Some individuals on the Right want to err on the side of what they consider efficient by eliminating the welfare system altogether. But a genuinely compassionate approach must begin by distinguishing between those programs that have worked and those that have failed. Obviously, programs that promote self-sufficiency should be retained and those that do not should either be dropped or modified.

Welfare policies must consider not just the goals, but the nature of the population they are intended to serve. For example, it is not enough to tell young children that if they work hard and behave, they will have a good job someday. For most, that reward is too remote. It would be better to find more immediate ways of rewarding our nation's children for demonstrating the principles of discipline, hard work, and perseverance. They cannot learn those lessons if all they can think about at school is how hungry they are. No child of America in 1996 should have to be hungry at school. If private initiative does not see to that, government can and must.

We question whether the desire to take government totally out of the welfare business, as some want to do, is based more on the goal of helping people in need or on the economic goal of lowering taxes. Traditionally, idealistic thinking has been considered a hallmark of the Left. But Ralph Reed bucks that conventional wisdom. He writes that if religious conservatives took their proper place in the society, government

> would be small because citizens and private institutions would voluntarily perform many of its functions. We would not need a large, bloated welfare state to take care of us, for we would take care of each other.... Through private initiatives and sound public policy, those who were hungry would be fed, those who were thirsty would drink, those who were homeless would be housed, and those who were hurting would be comforted.[10]

He continues, "Lower taxes would unleash the charitable capacity of the American people."[11] We are not convinced that things would fall so neatly into place. After all, charitable contributions decreased in the 1980s even with lower taxes.

What Reed describes may have been more likely to happen back in the 1950s. It was more common then for the wealthy to respond to the needs of the poor because they were more likely to live in the same communities. Responding to need was more personal. In contrast, over the last few decades, people of means, including evangelicals, have moved to wealthy subdevelopments and helped write zoning laws that have had the effect of keeping out poor people.

Our cultural values have changed, not just with regard to family values, but with regard to materialism and community responsibility. Baseball players are no longer content to be making more money than they could ever have imagined, more than they know how to spend. Nowadays, the goal is to make absolutely as much as possible. Today they spurn $2.1 million a year, holding out for $2.3 million. Last year Cal Ripken, Jr., was treated as a hero largely because he stood out by putting other values ahead of money.

Many people in this country are willing to understand and tolerate the federal deficit because, thanks to credit cards, they are "up to their ears" in debt themselves. Just a generation ago people would not consider "buying" something if they could not purchase it with cash. But not today, thanks to the lure of materialism.

Thus it is fair to ask how deep Americans' pockets will be as the responsibility for the poor shifts to the private sector. According to the *Washington Post,* faith-based organizations responded admirably to budget cuts during the early years of the Reagan administration. The *Post* reports, "The para-church organization Bread for the World estimates 150,000 churches now run emergency food or feeding programs. By 1991, according to the Yearbook of American and Canadian Churches, almost as many congregations offered services to the poor as offered religious education."[12] But according to Independent Sector, an umbrella organization of some 800 charities, per household giving between 1989 and 1993 dropped by 24 percent. And between 1991 and 1993, volunteerism declined 5 percent.[13]

As Arkansas Lieutenant Governor Mike Huckabee told the Christian Coalition, "Part of the reason that government has gotten too big and is trying to do things it was never intended to do ... is because some of us in the church who now complain about 50 cents of every one of our dollars going to support a bloating federal government are the same people who refused to give God one dime out of a dollar which should have been going to take care of the homeless, the hurting, and the helpless."[14]

We wonder whether times have truly changed. Giving in National Association of Evangelicals denominations has fallen from 6.72 percent in 1968 to 4.62 percent in 1992. *Christianity Today* reports that "evangelical churches are experiencing reduced giving" as a result of "materialism, individualism, and a younger, tithe-resistant generation."[15]

But a compassionate approach to welfare must go beyond a discussion of money. It must include a thorough effort to understand the reasons people get on and stay on welfare. It seems society can accept people who do not work because they suffer from some kind of physically debilitating condition such as cancer. But mental illness is less likely to be accepted as an excuse. This assumes that we know as much about mental illness as we ought to know in order to make fair distinctions between the so-called deserving and undeserving poor. Psychologists now maintain that some forms of depression have physiological roots. That being the case, people who suffer from depression may have legitimate reasons for not being able to earn a paycheck.

Upper-class individuals have no trouble acknowledging the reality of such conditions as Chronic Fatigue Syndrome, Carpal Tunnel Syndrome, or Temporomandibular Joint Disorder (TMJ). But when it comes to the poor, it seems that these are less likely to be accepted as excuses not to work. Who is "deserving" and who is "undeserving"? The truth is that in many cases, we do not know for sure. And, to make things worse, we may not know that we do not know. Amid this uncertainty and in accordance with the "Tenth Commandment" we proposed in chapter 5, we believe that our society must err on the side of granting welfare benefits to people until we know with absolute certainty that they are simply trying to avoid responsibility.

Many poor people avoid responsibility not because they want to, but because they never learned how to accept it. They are insecure. They fear the outside world for reasons those who have not "been there" have trouble understanding. They have no idea how to conduct themselves in a job interview. They have no nice clothes to wear, and perhaps would not even recognize what the business world considers appropriate clothing these days.

Some people are in this state of affairs because all they have known is poverty and welfare. Society bears some responsibility for that. They ought not simply to be cut off, and expected to go "cold turkey." They must be weaned. As a matter of principle, welfare benefits should be connected in some way to programs that can address the fundamental problems, programs that can provide the help that is needed. Among other things, this would ensure that money intended to support children does not end up supporting a drug habit.

Faith-based social service organizations are in an ideal position to provide the holistic care that can make a real difference in lives of people immersed in a culture of poverty. We call for government programs to cease discriminating against public service organizations that are motivated by Christian faith and values. Such discrimination is based on the misguided attempt to remain neutral with respect to religion. We reject this myth of neutrality.

We support the approach taken by U.S. Senator John Ashcroft of Missouri, who introduced the "Charitable Choice" provisions that were part of the Senate's welfare reform bill last year. The provisions, which ultimately failed to achieve approval of the full Congress, called for allowing Christian churches and other faith-based organizations to lay claim to government resources without having to suppress their religious character. A caring and efficient government should have a vested interest in supporting Christian social service programs, not because they promote religion, but because they work.

The legislation proposed by Ashcroft specified that government funds secured by private religious organizations should be used only for the social outreach programs for which they are intended. For those who are concerned about the separation of church and state, Ron Sider of Evangelicals for Social Action offers the perfect solution: vouchers. Sider proposes that those who need help from the government—whether medical attention, counseling for a drug problem or crisis pregnancy—be given vouchers. They would then be free to choose the program—faith-based or not—that is most likely to help them while respecting their religious beliefs. We can think of no good reason why policy makers should delay even for a day work on this approach to welfare reform.

In summary, as moderates we agree with many of the concerns conservatives have raised with regard to the welfare system. And yet we fear that their agenda is driven at points more by political and economic commitments than by concern for the poor. This is evident in the hard-line stand many on the Christian Right have taken against granting aid to women on welfare who get pregnant.

Pat Robertson and others on the Right contend that women have children in order to receive welfare benefits. This contention flies in the face of viewpoints of virtually all people, including Christian people, who are in the best position to know.

The idea that teenagers have babies to get welfare aid would be laughable if its consequences, including loss of life for unborn children, were not so serious. Rutgers University conducted a year-long study of some 5000 women on welfare. Half of them were subject to a "family cap" on aid if they got pregnant. The study found that the birth rates in the two groups were almost identical.[16] Says Kristin Moore, executive director of the Washington, D.C.-based research organization Child Trends, "Teens are not planners. They don't intend to become pregnant for any reason, much less planning to become pregnant so they can have a baby and go on welfare."[17] Speaking at the Christian Coalition's 1995 Road to Victory conference, former Pennsylvania Governor Robert Casey said, "In fact, there is no connection between benefit levels for children and out-of-wedlock births.... Family caps take food from children, increase poverty among women and families, and also encourage abortion." Activist Helen Alvare of the U.S. Catholic Conference and respected conservative thinker Glenn Loury are among those who say exactly the same thing.

Nevertheless, Gary Bauer of the Family Research Council supports the idea of a family cap, believing such a cap would discourage illicit sexual activity. "I may be unrealistic," he was quoted as saying in the *Washington Post*, "but I think ... sending that cultural message and ending the subsidies would influence behavior."[18] With all due respect, as moderates, we are unwilling to risk the lives of unborn children while Mr. Bauer wonders whether he is being realistic on this issue.

POINTS OF UNITY

Regardless of their positions on welfare policies, Christians should be able to agree that the church can and should be doing more to help poor people. Such help should be delivered in ways that enable the needy to become self-sufficient. In addition to serving the poor, the church should be proclaiming a gospel that challenges our culture's materialistic bent. On this point the Bible seems especially clear.

Chapter Ten

Abortion

Whatever you want to say about the anti-abortionists, you have got to at least say this: Theirs is the most disinterested act of humanitarian concern since the Emancipation Proclamation. They are not talking about protecting their own child, they are talking about protecting children.

William F. Buckley in an interview in *Christianity Today*[1]

Sociologist James Davison Hunter has suggested that abortion could be the catalyst for America's next civil war. No single issue divides the people of America quite so deeply as abortion, and it is no mystery as to why. On many other issues, the dividing line between the political Left and Right takes place at the level of analysis or interpretation of facts. But the gulf that divides our culture on the abortion issue is more fundamental than that. As we will explain below, for many this issue pits incompatible value systems, or worldviews, against one another.

While some political issues and attitudes divide the evangelical community, the issue of abortion constitutes a significant opportunity for unity among evangelicals. Many, if not most, evangelicals regard abortion as immoral and believe it should also be illegal. This does not mean evangelicals are of one mind on most aspects of the abortion question. As we will suggest below, moderates are less likely to separate the abortion discussion from a discussion of other cultural issues.

A MODERATE PERSPECTIVE

In his book *Cease Fire,* Tom Sine takes James Dobson to task for his virulent attacks on President Clinton. Sine explains that he wrote to Dobson, asking him to explain his anti-Clinton rhetoric. Dobson replied that it was based mainly on Clinton's position on abortion. Sine correctly points out that abortion is not the only pro-life issue; however, he treats abortion in a way that implies it is on par, in terms of its significance, with other issues such as world hunger and the environment. Without endorsing Dobson's treatment of the President, we generally support him in the belief that abortion is not just one more issue.

To his credit, Dobson has stood up not just to the President but to the Republican party as well. In an effort to build consensus for the sake of party unity, politicos within the GOP try to treat abortion simply as one among many issues, implying that people should compromise for the sake of the larger cause. This fails to recognize that, for many in the pro-life camp, abortion *is* the larger cause, or at least a central, indispensable part of that cause. Dobson has stated publicly that if the GOP tent is big and wide enough to include advocates of legal abortion, he would be looking for another tent.

Many political issues represent conflicting assessments based on the same goals and value systems. For example, most agree that eliminating world hunger and preserving the environment are worthy goals, although there is no consensus on the policies needed to achieve them. In contrast, the abortion debate reflects fundamental philosophical differences. It puts at issue the very moral foundations on which our society orders itself. Is the rightness or wrongness of abortion absolute—determined by something or someone outside ourselves? Or can abortion be right for some and wrong for others, based on personal religious values, as the pro-choice movement holds? How we answer this question as a culture has ramifications that extend far beyond the issue of abortion.

At one time the abortion debate focused mainly on the ques-

tion of whether a fetus is a human life or merely an inanimate mass. People supported legal abortion based on the view that a fetus was not really a life. Now, however, many in the pro-choice camp argue that abortion should be legal *even if* it constitutes the taking of innocent life. According to this argument, the value of life is no longer absolute. Unborn life is extinguishable if it poses a problem or inconvenience to those responsible for beginning that life.

Proponents of legal abortion routinely allege that conservatives care more about life in the womb than they do about life outside the womb. They contend that abortion prevents child abuse. But if abortion takes a human life, then abortion itself could be said to constitute the worst form of child abuse. Some in the pro-choice camp claim that it is hypocritical for people to oppose abortion if they are not willing to care for mothers who chose not to abort and care also for their children. That is like saying that people have no right to oppose burglary unless they are willing to find good-paying jobs for people who steal. It is like saying that we have no right to oppose drug abuse or drive-by shootings unless we are first willing to provide better recreational opportunities for wayward youth.

In any case, this charge against Christians is untrue. Thousands of crisis pregnancy centers across America work every day to provide tens of thousands of unwed mothers with material, emotional, and spiritual support. The knock on conservatives is that they are materialistic and selfish. Yet on the abortion issue they defy that stereotype. It is the abortion industry, not the pro-life movement, that has a vested economic interest in keeping abortion legal.

The moral relativism of the pro-choice movement is evidenced by Kate Michelman of the National Abortion Rights Action League. She maintains essentially that if a person believes abortion is wrong, it becomes wrong for him or her, but that no one has the right to say it is wrong for another person. Based on this logic, if a couple believes they are justified in taking the life of their infant child, who is to say they are wrong?

The answer to that question is, "Each and every American." We have established strict laws in our society against the taking of innocent human life. And Christian citizens, motivated by biblical faith, have the right and, we believe, the responsibility to argue in the public square that those laws should extend to unborn human life.

In efforts to persuade others, however, Christians should take care to use the Bible responsibly. After all, it does not directly address the issue of abortion. Quoting the psalmist who said that God knew him when he was still in the womb is an oft-used but irresponsible biblical argument against abortion. The literary genre of the Psalms is poetry, which is characterized by hyperbole and figures of speech intended to convey general impressions, and, in this case, God's omniscience. To use such passages as arguments against abortion sets a precedent that would allow virtually anything to be proved from Scripture.

Some base their anti-abortion views on the Sixth Commandment: "Thou shalt not kill" (KJV). But the Hebrew language had several words for the English word "kill." In the case of this commandment, the Hebrew word focuses on killing members of one's own family or clan. "You shall not murder" (NIV) captures even better the meaning of the Hebrew.

A passage from Exodus introduces ambiguity into the abortion debate. According to Hebrew law (Ex. 21:22), if two men are fighting and strike a pregnant woman, they are to be executed if she dies. But no one is punished if the woman merely loses her child through miscarriage as a result of the violence.

Given everything else the Bible says about protecting life, a pro-choice argument cannot stand on this one Old Testament passage any more than a pro-life argument can stand on a Psalm. The point is that Christians should use the Bible responsibly, recognizing that abortion is not specifically addressed in Scripture.

Some Christians, including evangelicals, find support in Scripture for the view that human life should not be defined strictly in biological terms, but in terms of relationship. Based on

this view, human life begins only when the fetus begins to move, which is when its relationship with another human being begins. Those who accept this view would still oppose all late-term abortions on biblical grounds.

As difficult as it might be on an emotional issue such as abortion, we urge evangelicals to consider our "Second Commandment" ("Thou shalt acknowledge that thy brother or sister may disagree with thee and yet remain deserving of thy respect as a brother or sister") and resist the temptation to define others' Christianity in terms of this issue. We should all be able to affirm that the Bible takes a high view of human life and consistently advocates protecting the weakest and most vulnerable. Based on this, it is reasonable to conclude that abortion is morally wrong.

We do not challenge the sincerity of Christian faith held by those, including President Clinton, who have arrived at a different position on abortion. The President has said he has agonized over the issue, as indeed many people have. He even concedes that he is uncertain when life begins. We appeal to him and others like him to reconsider their position, not based on our certainty but based on their own *lack* of certainty. In the midst of uncertainty, we urge people, in keeping with our "Tenth Commandment," to err on the side of the least moral risk. Speaking hypothetically, if the pro-choice movement is right—and abortion is not morally wrong—then many women (and men) have paid a high price in their fight for abortion rights. But if abortion is murder, then millions of innocent children have paid the ultimate price. Men and women who have contributed to a pregnancy have other options besides abortion. Unborn children do not.

Christians who believe that abortion constitutes the taking of innocent human life have the right and responsibility to support legislation outlawing abortion. But this point of view is not limited to people of faith. *Village Voice* columnist Nat Hentoff, an atheist and social liberal by almost any standard, views abortion as a civil rights issue and the act of abortion as a violation of the most fundamental right: the right to life.

The Rescue Movement and Violence

The emergence of the "rescue" response to abortion over the last decade or so has presented hundreds of thousands of pro-life Christians with a major dilemma. On the one hand, they believe that abortion is tantamount to murder, but on the other hand, participating in rescue efforts stands in tension with respect for the laws of the land.

Some people in the pro-life movement regard abortion merely as an issue and believe that once the issue is won, all will be well. The rescue approach of saving lives today highlights an important fact: For the millions of unborn children who will be denied the right to live, abortion is not just an interesting political debate but a matter of life and death. Operation Rescue and other organizations have rightly stressed that if abortions were to cease tomorrow, there should be no victory celebration, only remorse for a national tragedy. Based on this sense of urgency, the rescue movement has been a wakeup call for thousands of Christians to put their faith into action instead of just going through the motions.

Our concerns with the rescue movement are based on the rescue philosophy. As articulated by such leaders as Randall Terry, the rescue philosophy ultimately justifies violence.

One of the biggest mistakes the press has consistently made in its coverage of the rescue movement has been to portray it as civil disobedience. Though blocking the entrances to abortion clinics resembles the civil disobedience of the '60s, Terry and other rescue philosophers insisted from the beginning that Operation Rescue was *not* about civil disobedience. Civil disobedience entails breaking the law. Martin Luther King, Jr., recognized and respected the laws of the land, even though he believed some of those laws were immoral. He was willing to pay the price for breaking the law in order to raise society's moral consciousness. That is what civil disobedience is all about.

In contrast, Randall Terry does not regard rescue activities as civil disobedience. Again, civil disobedience entails breaking the law. But in the early days of the movement, Terry told rescuers

they were not breaking any laws. Instead, they were obeying God's higher law. The distinction may seem semantic, but in fact it is extremely significant. In this case, the emphasis on obeying God's higher law reflects the movement's roots in Reconstructionist (theocratic) thought. Indeed, at the rescue activities in Atlanta during the summer of 1988, most of the literature made available by Operation Rescue to explain its philosophy was written by Joseph Foreman, an avowed Reconstructionist. In remarks to the press, Terry cited Foreman as being the "brains" behind the movement.

At rescuer training sessions, Terry routinely compared rescue activity to ignoring a "No Trespassing" sign in order to save a drowning child. According to the law, he said no one can be arrested for trespassing to save a life. The law could be disregarded due to special circumstances. According to Terry, since saving a child from abortion also constitutes special circumstance, the laws protecting abortion clinics from disruption should be ignored.

The implications of this illustration are significant and telling. One could reasonably conclude that the law against striking another person can be disregarded if we strike that person in order to protect a child from being beaten. One could even conclude, as some have done, that someone is justified in taking the life of another person—such as shooting a doctor who performs abortions—in order to keep that person from murdering another human being. And Terry has never been hesitant to call abortion "murder."

Whereas Martin Luther King's civil disobedience was rooted in philosophical pacifism, Randall Terry's Operation Rescue was born out of "just war" principles, according to which violence is justified when one has no other options to protect the lives of the innocent. Says anti-abortion activist C. Roy McMillan, "It wouldn't bother me if every abortionist in the country today fell dead from a bullet."

For the record, Terry denounces violence, perhaps because it is expedient for him to do so. The truth is, however, that violence is a logical extension of his rescue philosophy. Those who have gone on to kill doctors or to bomb abortion clinics are merely

demonstrating their familiarity with Operation Rescue's foundational philosophy.

Many in the traditional pro-life movement like to think of the violent element as a radical fringe. Charles Colson resents the conclusion drawn by some in the media that considering abortion to be murder is tantamount to advocating violence. "Never mind," he writes, "that every responsible pro-life leader has repudiated the killings."[2]

Yet it is not hard to understand the perception that pro-life leaders have been too soft on the issue of abortion clinic violence. Some leaders typically do not categorically reject the violence, but instead link it to the violence of abortion. Said Flip Benham, Operation Rescue's currrent leader, "We will not have peace outside the womb until peace is restored in the womb."[3] Judie Brown of the American Life League was quoted as saying, "Whether it be by curette, by suction machine, or by bullets shot by a man who was obviously disturbed, the taking of a fellow human being's life is wrong."[4] Benham and Brown make valid points, but failing to condemn the violence without qualification risks sending the message to the perpetrators of abortion clinic violence that what they are doing is not all that bad.

In his monthly newsletter of January 1995, Dr. Dobson defended Randall Terry without reference to abortion clinic violence. Focus on the Family's January 5, 1995, edition of *Family Issues Alert* condemns "the use of violence against those who advocate abortion." It also reports the position of Operation Rescue as follows: "We deplore the actions of those who would pull a trigger rather than pick up the cross of Christ to defend the innocent." Again, we maintain that this stance cannot be reconciled with Operation Rescue's foundational philosophy.

As moderates, we encourage people at least to be cognizant of the logical implications of subscribing to the philosophy of Operation Rescue. We agree that Christians are called upon to protect innocent life. But in 1996, that stands in tension with the reality that abortion is legal. Tragic as that is, in the authors' judgment, the license to kill or do violence in accordance with

just war theory is limited to conscription in an organized army in wartime. Thus we support efforts to persuade government to strengthen laws against abortion, especially in cases where it is merely another means of birth control. And without qualification, we reject the violence against abortion clinics and doctors.

Abortion and Women's Rights

Pro-choice women view the issue of abortion within the context of a culture in which women have been dehumanized and victimized by means that include rape, domestic violence, and limited career opportunities. Abortion as an affirmation of women's "reproductive freedom" has come to represent the major battleground in their war against a society that—blatantly and subtly—treats women as inferior. Thus abortion for some is not just a choice, but a statement.

The church has contributed to the perception of women as inferior. Many theological conservatives who are part of the pro-life movement maintain that the Bible decrees designated roles for males and females in the church, in the family, and in society at large. The practical result is that men are the decision makers and women are the followers. Men may preach at church, but women may not. Men are spared from changing dirty diapers or getting up in the middle of the night with a sick child, because that is women's work. As evangelical scholar and author Gretchen Gaebelein Hull has documented, some men in the church have even found biblical grounds for physical punishment of their wives.[5]

Pro-life Christians would have more credibility on the abortion issue if they were more committed to advocating women's rights in other social arenas. Obviously, we cannot expect people—in order to score points in the abortion debate—to disregard what they believe Scripture teaches about distinct male and female roles. (In fact, many fundamentalists maintain that support for women's rights [i.e., feminism] is part of the same secular humanist ideology that supports legalized abortion.)

Perhaps there was a time when advocates—whether male or

female—of Christian feminism were by definition theologically liberal. But if there was such a time, it is now past. Individuals such as Lewis Smedes, Cline Snodgrass, Gilbert Bilezikian, Ron Sider, and Mary Stewart Van Leeuwen are among the many evangelical scholars who uphold the Bible as God's authoritative word but who have reached a different conclusion on gender roles dictated by Scripture. Given the sheer number of respected evangelical scholars who regard women as being equally responsible for leadership in the church and home, we urge opponents of this view to consider whether their position owes more to tradition and habit than to biblical truth.

Van Leeuwen points out that

> when we look at that great passage from the creation account in Gen. 1:26–28—the passage containing what Reformed theologians often call the "cultural mandate" to humankind—we do not find God saying to the first female, "Be fruitful and multiply," and to the first male, "Subdue the earth." On the contrary, *both* are called to accountable dominion and to accountable sociability and fruitfulness: "And God blessed *them* and said to *them,* 'Be fruitful and multiply, and fill the earth and subdue it. . . .'" There is no warrant here for rigidly-separate spheres or activities based on gender: both women and men, made in the image of God, are called to unfold the potential of creation in all areas of life, to engage in good, stewardly and God-honoring activities *together*, whether those activities take place close to the hearth, within the worship setting, or elsewhere in the social and natural world.[6]

Many Christian feminists, represented by such organizations as Feminists For Life, oppose abortion while upholding the full equality of women. We urge moderates to recognize and celebrate their efforts. To the extent that evangelical moderates advance the view of women as equal partners with men, we can make progress toward the goal of recasting the abortion issue as an issue primarily about life, not about women's rights.

Working with "the Enemy"

If the result of making abortion illegal is to steer desperate women in the direction of unlawful abortion, the victory is shallow. The ultimate goal of the pro-life movement is not to criminalize abortion, but to prevent abortions from taking place. Accomplishing that goal will require efforts to change society's moral consciousness one individual at a time.

Some have resorted too quickly to the weapons of cultural war, believing that the enemy is beyond hope. The fact that Operation Rescue's Flip Benham struck up a friendship with Norma McCorvey, the "Jane Roe" of *Roe v. Wade* fame, suggests that anyone's heart and mind can change.

Thus, in addition to legal activity, we support efforts to change society's moral consciousness on abortion. Doing that entails taking seriously the biblical injunction to love our enemies. We must, with compassion, realize that many feel incapable of facing the prospect that abortion is morally wrong because the guilt from that would be too overwhelming. We must remind people that nothing anyone has done or can do is outside the boundaries of God's redemptive love and forgiveness.

We also urge Christians to build bridges with their ideological opponents. If it can be done on the abortion issue, it can be done on any issue. And we believe it can be done. Pro-choice and pro-life people share the goal of preventing unwanted pregnancies. Even though they disagree at some points about how to accomplish this, it is at least a starting point.

Emphasizing the adoption option is another area where opponents on the abortion issue might find common ground. Former Pennsylvania Governor Robert Casey maintains that adoption should be made a top national priority. He says that President Clinton should be able to pick up the phone and call Newt Gingrich and say, "We disagree on a lot of things, but there is one thing we agree on, and that is that foster care, despite all the heroes and heroines in that movement, doesn't work for most children. It's the most anti-child and the most expensive alternative in

the whole child care system."[7] Adoption could help resolve this problem, although it may not be a panacea.

Working together represents the best hope that children, born and unborn, will be treated as they should be. That is a far better option than allowing them to become victims of cultural warfare.

POINTS OF UNITY

All Christians should be able to agree that the safest moral path is to avoid abortion wherever possible. This includes working toward the elimination of unwanted pregnancies. They should also take a strong, unequivocal stand against violence toward abortion clinics. And even if they disagree about what the Bible says about women's roles, Christians should unite to the extent possible in standing against the denigration of women.

Chapter Eleven

"Family Values"

What America needs most at this point ... is not a set of new
programs, but people of conviction and tenacity who will say,
"This is my home, this is my neighborhood, this is my community.
I will do what I can to ... restore it, to rebuild."

U.S. Senator Dan Coats of Indiana at the
Christian Coalition's 1995 Road to Victory conference

In 1992 Vice President Dan Quayle, with a little help from Murphy Brown, put the issue of "family values" on the national map. He spoke up for the values associated with traditional families. According to those values, sex—and the children that go with it— are to be reserved for monogamous marriage between a man and a woman. And when the couple encounters difficulties, instead of rushing off to divorce court, they should work through their problems based on their commitment to each other and to the family. When these commitments are respected, children grow up in a stable environment, benefiting from the maturity, wisdom, and financial resources of two parents, instead of one.

The position held by Barbara Bush was not so definitive. When it came to family values, based on some of what she said, it seems she was not so sure whether Dan Quayle was right. "However you define family," the First Lady proffered in one speech, "that's what we mean by family values."[1]

A MODERATE PERSPECTIVE

Although he was lampooned by the press, Quayle accomplished his stated purpose of launching a discussion about values in this country. As evangelical moderates, we applaud him for this, and we reject Barbara Bush's notion that family values can mean whatever a person wants them to mean. We affirm the traditional evangelical conviction that a family is based on a monogamous relationship between a man and a woman.

Many evangelical scholars, including New Testament scholar Thomas E. Schmidt, have thoroughly articulated the biblical basis for this position. In his book *Straight and Narrow,* in which he addresses the question of homosexuality, Schmidt makes a strong case, based on Old and New Testament sources, that male-female monogamy constitutes God's moral norm. He writes, "The creation story in Genesis serves as a basis for biblical commands and subsequent reflection on human sexuality. Scripture teaches, and reason and tradition confirm, that heterosexual marriage is not only good, but exclusively good."[2]

In recent decades, the institution of marriage has faced tough times. Most would agree that divorce is sometimes the best option, especially in cases of physical abuse. But when over 40 percent of marriages end in divorce, something is wrong. When one in three babies are born out of wedlock, something is wrong. When half of our children spend at least some time prior to age 18 in a single-parent home, something is wrong.[3]

Every year, over a million children of America must deal with the divorce of their parents. According to the 1995 study *Marriage in America: A Report to the Nation,* the United States has gone from being the most marrying society in the world to being the society with the most divorces and unwed mothers.[4]

It used to be argued that lack of income, not single-parent family structure, was mainly responsible for putting children at risk, given the high correlation between low income and single parenthood. But thanks in part to the work of researchers such as Sara McLanahan and Gary Sandefur, both of whom identify with

the ideological Left, it is clear that children from single-parent homes across the board are worse off than those of similar economic status who have two parents. McLanahan and Sandefur state that "adolescents who have lived apart from one of their parents during some period of childhood are twice as likely to drop out of high school, twice as likely to have a child before age twenty, and one and a half times as likely to be 'idle'—out of school and out of work—in their late teens and early twenties."[5]

In 1994, according to the Annie E. Casey Foundation, 19 million children (24 percent) lived in homes without fathers present.[6] In 1950 that figure was only 6 percent. According to the foundation, boys who grow up without fathers are "much more likely to become incarcerated, unemployed, and uninvolved with their own children when they become fathers."[7]

The *Philadelphia Inquirer* reports that "because of crack cocaine, poverty, death and illness, more and more grandparents in the United States are caring for grandchildren without the benefit of the child's parents—723,000 grandparents raising more than 1.1 million grandchildren."[8]

Make no mistake about it: These embarrassing and tragic national statistics represent a decline in the moral values prescribed by Scripture. As a society and as individuals, we have made choices that are morally wrong and that have placed millions of our children at risk in many ways.

Many of those who would not listen to Dan Quayle did listen to Barbara Dafoe Whitehead, author of the widely recognized *Atlantic Monthly* article "Dan Quayle was Right." Whitehead has called attention to a pervasive shift from a child-centered to an adult-centered culture. It began in the 1960s, she says, as parents' happiness and potential for self-actualization began to take precedence over the safety and emotional stability of this country's most innocent citizens: children.[9]

This shift is reflected in a greeting card from Hallmark Cards on the occasion of divorce. The card reads: "Think of your former marriage as a record album. It was full of music, both happy and

sad. But what's important now is YOU, the recently released HOT NEW SINGLE. You're going to be at the top of the charts!"[10]

Whitehead makes the further observation that many people—from sociologists to educators to politicians—were hesitant to talk about the problem of divorce because *they* were themselves divorced.[11]

We reject the negativism of those who say this trend is irreversible. Individuals can change as can societies. When Dr. C. Everett Koop used his bully pulpit as Surgeon General to discourage people from smoking, many listened. Likewise, as both conservatives and liberals inform us about innocent victims of family disintegration, we should expect that more people will work harder to fulfill their wedding vows and their responsibilities as parents.

From a Christian point of view, the surest path to restoring family values is spiritual conversion and the moral commitment that accompanies it. Of course, this cannot be legislated. Yet Christians operating in the political arena have the right and responsibility to advocate public policies that reward, rather than discourage, ethical behavior and that support intact families.

As moderate evangelicals, we, like the Christian Right, oppose tax and welfare policies that provide incentives for families to break up rather than stay together. We reject granting "domestic partners" the same tax advantages enjoyed by legally married men and women. We agree with the Religious Right's support of tax incentives for adoption and a tax credit for families with elderly dependents. We hear the point behind former Pennsylvania governor Robert Casey's question when he asks, "Why is the money that you spend to feed and educate and clothe your children called 'consumption' and therefore taxable, but if you put the money in a building or machinery, that's called 'investment'?" He continues, "I believe investments in children and education—taking care of and raising kids, and creating strong families—are a lot more important to the long-term progress of this country than machines or buildings."[12]

Unfortunately, many on the Christian Right routinely define "traditional family" in ways that conform to stereotypes of males

as breadwinners and leaders and of women as homemakers and followers. According to psychologist Mary Stewart Van Leeuwen, when conservatives

> claim to be supporting the "traditional" family, the implicit dichotomies they assume between public and private, waged workplace and home, breadwinning father and domesticated mother (which both promote as unchanging and/or desirable norms of family life) are, in the long sweep of history, anything but "traditional." They are adaptations which occurred largely in response to the 19th century Industrial Revolution and the urbanization trends that accompanied it. Prior to that time, and notwithstanding the norm of patriarchal authority, gender roles overlapped considerably, and the traditional family was one in which workplace, dwelling place, and childrearing space co-existed for both men and women.[13]

Community Values

In our assessment of "family values," however, we part paths with the Religious Right not over what *has* been said (or assumed), but over what has been left unsaid. We contend that the Right's discussion of values has been limited, too focused on the family, as it were. We propose a broader discussion of cultural values, a discussion that adds, among other things, community values to the agenda.

The Bible has at least as much to say about our responsibilities to a community of people as it does about our responsibilities to a nuclear family. According to some scholars, the Bible defines "family" in terms of community. Theologian Cain Hope Felder points out that "the earliest traditions in the New Testament—those of Jesus and Paul—do not contain much elaboration on families or households based on blood kinship."[14] Felder suggests that "while the nuclear family is commendable in some respects,

neither in biblical times nor today can discussions of family life be restricted to the nuclear family model."[15]

Tom Sine writes, "You won't find anything in the Bible that supports the idolatrous preoccupation with protecting the individual biological family that characterizes many conservative Christian groups today. Read the New Testament again. There is very little mention of family. There is certainly nothing in the Bible about protecting the family as it is."[16]

Instead, the Bible emphasizes the spiritual kinship of believers and a commitment to community that follows from that. We hear a lot about the crisis of family values, but far too little about the crisis of community values. This crisis was illustrated a few years ago in the widely reported case of a woman who was dead for several weeks before her neighbors even knew it. Someone came to mow her grass and collect her mail. But no one knew her well enough to suspect something might be wrong.

In cities across this country, thousands of people—most of them elderly—died during the heat wave during the summer of 1995 in essence because of a lack of community: the absence of family, friends, or neighbors committed to looking after the needs of society's most vulnerable. Meanwhile, the oft-repeated African proverb "It takes a community to raise a child" is pooh-poohed by some conservatives, or worse, treated as an anti-family statement, as was the case with a guest on Focus on the Family's radio show last year.[17]

Loren Mead observes that church congregations "have been part of the social glue that de Tocqueville described as characteristic of this nation. They have been a center of community life."[18] Most contemporary churches, however, have abandoned the parish concept, have lost sight of the vital role they play in communities. People leave their communities to attend church across town or in another town. Personal preference for a particular church takes precedence over community commitment.

There was a time when "neighborhood watches" did not have to be created; they were a natural part of community living. Peo-

ple looked out for one another. They protected their neighbors' property, as well as the safety of their neighbors' children.

Writer Stanley Crouch was reared in the 1950s without a father, but everyone in his African-American community took responsibility for him and all other youth. He remembers the church women in his community reminding him that the Lord would help him if he studied his books. Even winos admonished him to study and stay out of trouble so he wouldn't end up like them. When he got his report card from school, he would take it around the neighborhood. People gave him 50 cents for Bs and a dollar for As.[19]

Family values cannot be separated from communities. Indeed, families, including Christian families, have been affected by a decline in community values in ways many of us do not even realize. There was a time when most children, in addition to a mother and father, had access to grandparents, aunts and uncles, long-time friends, schoolteachers, and other respected community leaders. As many a frustrated parent has discovered, teenagers are prone to ignore advice from Mom or Dad. But when they get the same advice from a grandparent or an older friend in the community, they are more likely to take it to heart.

Deprived of the resources offered by the extended family and the larger community, children and youth these days are increasingly forced to go it alone. The divorce rate is so high in part because of marriages that should never have taken place in the first place. That is bound to happen when young people have no access to the advice of those who are older and wiser, those who in previous generations had the opportunity to transmit their years of collective wisdom—on topics such as dating and marriage—to those who could benefit from it. Sociologist Emile Durkheim maintains that this society's epidemic of violence is due in part to the social upheaval that results from being disconnected from moral community.[20]

Today, in this culture of mobility, many Christian fathers and mothers don't think twice about uprooting their families every few years for a job that pays more or offers a better career opportunity.

Geographical mobility is often a prerequisite for upward mobility. Though this is certainly not as serious as divorce, this also takes away resources of support from young people that previous generations of youth enjoyed. We do not mean to suggest that all such moves are inherently immoral. We do, however, challenge parents to weigh their "need" for self-actualization or for a bigger house against what is best for the family. Unfortunately, few if any conservatives have offered a serious moral critique of our materialistically driven culture of mobility.

The Fifties: A Golden Age?

We do take issue with one additional aspect of conservatives' treatment of traditional family values. Without making reference to the moral progress achieved by the civil rights movement, Ralph Reed says he wants America to "look much like it did for most of the first two centuries of its existence, before the social dislocation caused by Vietnam, the sexual revolution, Watergate, and the welfare state."[21]

Unfortunately, many conservative leaders cannot talk about traditional values without mentioning *Leave It to Beaver* or reflecting on how great life was back in the fifties. They would have us believe that all we have to do is turn back the cultural clock about 40 years and life would be grand once again.

This is the implied message of the August 1995 cover of *Focus on the Family* magazine, which features a black-and-white photo of Ward Cleaver and family along with the words, "June and Ward Were Right." (The article inside expounds on the relationship between traditional family values and individual fulfillment and cultural stability.)

For the record, it is not necessary to go all the way back to the fifties to find examples of traditional family values. They can be found in such shows of the nineties as *Home Improvement, Step by Step, Christy, The Cosby Show, Sister, Sister,* and *Dr. Quinn, Medicine Woman.* Evangelical Christians contribute significantly to the production of at least three of these programs: *Step by Step,*

Christy, and *Home Improvement.* Unlike the Cleaver family, some of the television families of the nineties even go to church and believe in prayer.

By wanting to return to the "Golden Age" of the 1950s, conservatives needlessly offend many of those in our society for whom life, in some important ways, was not so grand in the 1950s. For example, African-Americans would be loathe to turn back the clock to pre-civil rights days. They remember the fifties as an age in which an entire race of God's people experienced open, blatant discrimination. Meanwhile, the Cleavers reaped the benefits of the white, privileged middle class. Content to represent the status quo, they had no black friends. On that count, June and Ward were wrong.

We suspect that some conservatives are loathe to cite more contemporary expressions of family values because of the messages they communicate regarding women's roles in the culture and family. In all of the shows of the nineties cited above, women are regarded as equals. The programs advance an egalitarian, rather than a hierarchical, arrangement between husband and wife. In contrast, although Ward helped dry the dishes and June was not exactly barefoot and pregnant, it was always clear who "wore the pants" in the Cleaver family: Ward. He brought home the proverbial bacon while June cleaned house, albeit in earrings and a dress.

David Elkind, professor of child study at Tufts University, maintains that this women-belong-in-the-home mentality helps explain our society's high divorce rate.[22] He calls attention to the heavy use of tranquilizers among frustrated middle-class mothers in the 1950s. Instead of turning back the clock, he advocates working toward balancing the needs of parents and children.

Many conservative pro-family organizations advocate a hierarchical view of the family, with the father being primarily responsible for leadership in the home. Not all such organizations, it should be noted, are monolithic in terms of their stance on gender roles. For example, Promise Keepers and Focus on the Family advocate a hierarchical model. But they advocate such high

respect and commitment to women that it is unfair to lump them into the same category as everyone else.

Unfortunately, the hierarchical model of family organization has often been translated in ways that grant males privileged status. Dad goes off to work and off to the golf course while Mom stays home to wash clothes and change dirty diapers. And when there is a disagreement, Dad gets his way.

As discussed in chapter 8, to hold the view that men and women should be equal partners in the home, church, and society can no longer simply be written off as being theologically liberal. Many evangelical scholars support this view. In fact, although he advocates male headship in the home, James Dobson is a faithful member of the Church of the Nazarene, which supports women's ordination.

Ultimately, both sides in this debate cannot be right. According to God's design, either the male should be in charge or male and female were meant to function as equal partners. If the male should be head of the household, then conservatives are likely correct in blaming family breakdown on strident feminism and the failure of husbands to assume their proper leadership roles. On the other hand, if the Bible teaches that both males and females should serve as joint leaders, then the conservative viewpoint is likely placing needless stress on women and families. It may actually be contributing to divorce. We encourage Christians to examine the latest scholarship and to reach a decision on this issue based on the biblical evidence, not on tradition.

In summary, as moderates, we encourage a broad discussion of cultural values, one that includes, but is not dominated by, a narrow focus on the family. We encourage all people to recognize the price this country has paid by losing sight of the importance of community. After all, the Bible does not dictate exactly what constitutes a family. It does, however, make clear that we owe responsibilities toward our parents and children, husbands and wives, sisters and brothers, friends and neighbors, and even our enemies.

We encourage believers not to forsake the values inherent in

community living for purposes of selfish individualism. Recognizing that making a lifelong commitment to a community should in no way be considered a moral absolute, we encourage Christians to work at creating and building community wherever they find themselves. This entails everything from taking a fatherless child to a ball game to shoveling snow for the elderly couple down the street. Getting to know others entails a certain amount of risk, but it also opens doors to personal enrichment and to the enhancement of the kinds of family values that would make Dan, June, and Ward proud.

POINTS OF UNITY

Christians should be able to find unity in their support of public policies, including tax-related policies, that strengthen families. They should affirm together that the Bible speaks extensively about our responsibilities to communities and should explore together ways in which they might uphold community values.

Chapter Twelve

The Justice System

The biblical teaching on justice does not call for simply warehousing criminals. It calls for restoring the peace—the shalom—of the community.

Charles Colson[1]

If the crime rate of a society fairly reflects the adequacy of its justice system, the United States is struggling. Our homicide rate is 17 times greater than Japan's or Ireland's. It is 10 times higher than the murder rates in Germany, France, or Greece, and five times higher than Canada's.[2] The homicide rate for teenage males is at an all-time high. According to the FBI, the 1994 violent crime rate (murder, rape, aggravated assault, and robbery) was 7.2 per 1000 people.[3]

According to the U.S. Justice Department, one out of 140 adults is in prison. That's more than one million people, twice as many as were incarcerated just a decade or so ago. More college-age African-American men are in prison than in college.

When it comes to reforming the justice system, getting "tough on crime" has become the rallying cry for politicians from both major parties. Support for capital punishment is high and on

the rise. The most strident conservatives have lost all sight of the prison system's role in rehabilitating men and women. Their rhetoric suggests they have little or no desire to understand the circumstances that help put people behind bars. They are interested only in keeping criminals as far away from law-abiding citizens for as long as possible.

Meanwhile, some of those on the Left want to blame crime almost exclusively on such social pathologies as racism and economic injustice or on bad parenting. Clearly, our society is suffering from a crisis of personal accountability wherein more and more people, with the help of slick and unprincipled lawyers, claim they are not responsible for their actions, however violent or immoral.

A MODERATE PERSPECTIVE

The urge to get tough on crime is understandable in this age where violence has reached epidemic proportions and where more and more people across this country are living in fear, feeling imprisoned in their own homes and neighborhoods. But if getting tough is just a reaction, rather than thoughtful action, it can result in unintended, negative results. As Prison Fellowship and other reform-minded groups have pointed out, the tougher we get on nonviolent offenders, the less room there is in prisons for those who are the most dangerous.

Building bigger prisons is the easiest solution and the most popular one among politicians, who increasingly espouse a "lock-the-door-and-throw-away-the-key" mentality. Not only does this mean more government spending, but it militates against the goal of reforming people and helping them to become productive members of society. Philosophically, this approach flies in the face of the Christian concept of grace. The grace of God is about second chances, not dead ends. This does not mean that crime should go unpunished. It does mean that those who commit crimes should not be forgotten forever. Let us not forget how God worked in the lives of murderers—such as Moses and the apostle Paul.

We encourage those who are in a position to reform our justice system to think not primarily about getting tougher on crime, but about getting smarter about crime. This entails moving away from an exclusive emphasis on punishment and toward exploring the "three R's": reconciliation, restitution, and rehabilitation. This approach, we believe, is not just a higher moral road, but a more pragmatic approach over the long haul. Prison Fellowship and its affiliated organization, Justice Fellowship, have been attempting to communicate this message for years.

An emphasis on reconciliation recognizes that, while the justice system is impersonal, crime is a very personal thing. It affects both victim and offender psychologically, emotionally, and spiritually. Reconciliation and restitution represent the opportunity for both the victim and the offender to heal the damage that has been done and to redeem the situation for good.

We recognize that some offenders are beyond hope of being reformed short of God's miraculous intervention and that some victims are too angry and bitter even to consider an effort at reconciliation. Yet too few options exist within the system's current structure for those who do want to seek healing through reconciliation.

Likewise, rehabilitation represents the opportunity for convicts to reshape their lives and to make better choices in the future. Tough-on-crime politicians want to eliminate prison weight rooms and various other recreational opportunities within prisons. Some of them make it sound as if prison is a fun place to be. Ironically, those who are lifting weights are generally the model prisoners, the "points of light," the ones who represent the best hope for the prison system to work as it should. To deprive them of motivation represents the ultimate abandonment of the rehabilitative approach.

An exclusive emphasis on punishment unmasks a society bent on the unbiblical desire for vengeance. Perhaps we have mistakenly equated vengeance and justice. Justice has to do with punishment for violating laws for the purpose of maintaining order in society. Vengeance has to do with hatred and contempt for offenders. Not only is it possible, but it is necessary for us as a society to maintain justice without fostering vengeance.

That attitude is modeled by Sue Norton, who regularly visits and exchanges letters with the man on death row accused of killing both of her parents in 1990.[4] Through the witness of her Christian faith, this man has personally accepted the message of Christ's redemptive love and forgiveness. Sue Norton realized that healing from her pain was more likely to come by pursuing reconciliation rather than giving in to feelings of vengeance. Crime victims who seek healing through vengeance are as misguided as the addict who finds fulfillment through drugs. According to the Bible, vengeance belongs to God.

A Call for Consistency

Part of being smart on crime is the recognition that the most important ingredient in any society's justice system is not toughness, but consistency. A punishment has the potential to work as a deterrent only when people know exactly what the consequences of their misbehavior will be. Proponents of capital punishment contend that the death penalty has not functioned as a deterrent because it has not been applied swiftly and consistently.

The inconsistencies of our justice system have been well documented by legal experts. Sentences vary from region to region, based largely on the whims of judges, the rhetorical skills of lawyers, the makeup of juries, and politics. But to give a detailed examination of these inconsistencies is beyond the purpose of this book.

One inconsistency we will address, however, pertains to race. This country's racial fault lines were exposed once again by the verdict in the O. J. Simpson trial. What each of us thought about this verdict reveals a lot about ourselves, specifically our fears. Many women were stunned and disappointed by the verdict because their greatest fear is to be oppressed and beaten by men. White people were dismayed because they fear that black criminals will come into their neighborhoods to kill and rob them.

Most of us concluded that a black jury would never convict a black defendant, even though during that same time span a mostly African-American jury convicted black Congressman Mel Reynolds of Illinois of having illicit sex with a teenage campaign worker.

Many African-Americans in this country were just as stunned as white people by the Simpson verdict. But the difference is that they were relieved, not disappointed. In spite of the outcome, they remain hostages of their greatest fear: They cannot find justice within the system.

Those of us who find this fear unreasonable should attempt to view things from the vantage point of the typical African-American. While white parents often tell their children to find a policeman if they are lost or in trouble, many black parents warn their children to steer clear of police because a policeman may not have their best interests in mind.

Through the years, many whites have had trouble believing the accounts of African-Americans who said that their people were routinely abused by police. Surely some frustrated black people must have thought, "If only we could get it on tape." And then, in 1992, someone did get it on tape. But it didn't matter. It was not enough to convict the Los Angeles police officers who were accused of beating Rodney King. Is it any wonder that some African-Americans would conclude that the current system holds no hope? The Simpson verdict, even for those who believe O. J. committed the crimes, represented hope.

We recognize that differences of opinion exist among evangelicals about how serious the problem of racism is in our justice and law enforcement systems. But let us not be so naïve as to believe that, now that Mark Fuhrman is gone from the Los Angeles Police Department, racism has been excised from police forces across the nation. We encourage fellow white Christians to research this issue for themselves by seeking the perspectives and opinions of black Christians. Go to the city and meet with African-American pastors or laypersons. Make sure they are conservative: staunchly pro-life and opposed to affirmative action, perhaps even registered Republicans. Ask these brothers and sisters in Christ, whom you have no reason not to trust, to tell you what they think about how racism affects the justice system. Let their answers influence your political viewpoints.

Accountability Crisis

In this day and age it is refreshing for someone to say, "I did it. It was my fault. I take responsibility. I deserve to be punished." Refreshing, but rare. These days, it seems that it's always someone else's fault: parents, drugs, mental illness, or the devil. It used to be when someone spilled hot coffee on their lap, it was their fault, not the fault of the person who made the coffee.

The extent to which individuals bear responsibility for their own actions has been debated by theologians for centuries. The contemporary debate revolves around complex theological, psychological, and physiological questions. There are no easy answers.

The Reformed doctrine of predestination was never intended to deny that human beings are responsible for their actions. Christian teaching on moral behavior presumes that people are capable of choosing good or evil. In his book *Straight and Narrow*, Thomas E. Schmidt admits that it is "natural" for him to have thoughts about having sex with women he's never met. He wonders where those feelings come from, whether he was born with them or whether culture has something to do with it. But he affirms that these kinds of questions are not moral questions: "Moral questions have to do with the rightness and wrongness of my actions, regardless of the source or strength of my desires."[5] He goes on to explain that it may very well be "unnatural" for a pedophile to seek a meaningful relationship with an adult or for some men to be faithful to their wives. But again, moral behavior has to do with making right choices, regardless of what seems natural.

Yet we cannot deny that for some people, making the right choice is more difficult than it is for others. Mental illness and a bad upbringing may not deprive people of genuine moral agency, but neither should these contributing factors be ignored. Old Testament law pertaining to capital punishment takes into consideration extenuating circumstances. We should do the same when evaluating what is behind aberrant behavior.

According to a recent study, 75 percent of violent, incarcerated youth suffered abuse by a family member and 78 percent had witnessed extreme violence.[6] According to statistics cited by Princeton University professor John J. Dilulio, Jr., more than half of all youths "in long-term state juvenile institutions have one or more immediate family members (father, mother, sibling) who have been incarcerated."[7] A child with a drug-abusing parent is four times as likely to become a drug abuser.[8]

Also, a clear connection exists between chances for success and being reared in a stable family. As Dilulio puts it, from the statistics, "one can see that being born healthy to loving parents of whatever income is about the luckiest accident that can befall a human being."[9]

Most people are saddened and outraged upon hearing stories of children being physically or sexually abused. Our hearts go out to these innocent and defenseless victims who are deprived of the opportunity for normal emotional, social, and spiritual growth. But when these same victims reach that magical age of accountability and treat others as they were treated, society loses all sight of their status as victims.

A tension exists between affirming personal responsibility on the one hand and acknowledging the reality of contributing social and psychological factors on the other. As the chief administrator at the Camden County (N.J.) Youth Center (a juvenile detention facility), Mary Previte has lived with this tension daily for more than 20 years. She knows that children are not born violent. They learn it. In her book *Hungry Ghosts,* she writes of "children robbed of their childhood. They steal. They sell their bodies—sell drugs—to manage a life of daily catastrophes. ... Sometimes what you do in a day," she observes, "is not as important as what you *undo*."[10]

In her book, Previte's struggle with the tension between responsibility and circumstances is obvious. At one point she discusses a rule she has at the Youth Center: "There are always consequences for everything you do. Good consequences. Bad consequences. Your choice."[11] But at another place, in reflecting on a particularly troubled youth, she asks, "Would I myself have come up short without the special attention—yes, and love—of people around me?"[12] She writes of children who suppress the emotions from the horror they have witnessed in what psychiatrists call "creative survival": "At the Youth Center we see the rage speaking in other voices—depression, headaches, wetting beds, sucking thumbs—little voices saying, Can you see me? Can you *listen*?"[13]

A Proactive Approach

To stress either personal responsibility or extenuating circumstances at the expense of the other is to claim certainty and to deny a mystery that ought not be denied. As a matter of principle, we must insist that people are responsible for their behavior, yet we must not summarily dismiss the importance of mitigating factors.

Acknowledging this tension between circumstances and moral responsibility makes a practical difference in how the church responds to those who have committed illegal or immoral acts. If we cast their struggles exclusively in terms of moral willpower, our response is limited to telling people that God hates sin, so they should "Just say no." This simplistic approach explains why people are flocking to 12-step programs instead of churches to seek healing. It's just not as easy as saying no. Unfortunately, psychological counseling, if not opposed as unspiritual, is still taboo in many Christian circles.

A proactive approach to helping people in need enables us to acknowledge both prongs of the dialectic: personal responsibility and mitigating factors. It is rooted in the belief that it is better to prevent crime than to punish crime, just as preventing heart disease is preferable to bypass surgery.

Creating economic opportunities is one way Christians—and society—can take a proactive approach to crime. Urban activist Jawanza Kunjufu tells the story of an encounter he had with an urban youth who sold drugs for a living.[14] Hoping to convince the young man that there was no future in what he was doing, Kunjufu asked him if he knew anyone who had been selling drugs for 10 years. The boy replied that they're all "dead, in prison, or strung out on drugs." Then Kunjufu warned the boy that he would probably end up the same. But the youth replied, "I'd rather end up like that than go back to where I came from."

A choice to sell drugs can in no way be considered moral. Yet it is not hard to understand, especially since profiting on some addictive and life-taking drugs, such as cigarettes, is perfectly legal and considered acceptable. It is even endorsed by U.S. Senators, including Jesse Helms.

People struggle to lay claim to their piece of the American pie in the absence of educational and economic opportunities. Their search for the good life does not justify breaking the law. But we would be naïve to deny a connection between crime and the lack of opportunity to succeed by the rules. A proactive approach entails improving the quality of choices for young people and for disenfranchised people in general. Not only is this approach more compassionate, but it is more pragmatic if the goal is to make this country a safer place. It does not negate the view that living simply is a virtue in this materialistic culture. But living simply should be a choice, not a necessity.

Finally, a proactive approach to crime entails the development of a thoughtful and thorough critique of violence. As mentioned in chapter 6, despite all the praises de Tocqueville heaped on America in the 1830s, he noticed its propensity for violence. We need more people in this country to be half as fascinated and intrigued by peace as they are by war. We need more churches and community organizations to sponsor seminars on topics such as "How to Deal with Anger" and "How to Channel Aggression." We need to learn and apply what the Bible teaches about violence and its personal and social causes.

In twentieth-century America, the propensity for violence is evidenced in part by an obsession with guns. As of this writing, there are over 200 million guns in circulation. In 1987 the U.S. toy industry spent over $40 million advertising new war toys, including water-and-dye pellet versions of the Uzi and AK–47.[15] Gunshot wounds are the leading cause of death for teenage boys in America.[16] According to one New Jersey medical examiner, it is cheaper to educate youth than to bury them, since an autopsy costs $2,500 and a homicide investigation can run up to $50,000.[17]

In 1990, handguns killed 22 people in Great Britain, 68 in Canada, 87 in Japan, and 10,567 in the United States.[18] In this culture of violence, we question the moral wisdom of the Christian Coalition giving booth space at its Road to Victory conferences to the National Rifle Association and *Moody Monthly* magazine giving advertising space to a gun repair business.[19]

Finally, while we affirm the right to own guns, we maintain that applying the Constitution to the issue of gun control represents a failure to understand the Constitution in its historical context. The right to bear arms was affirmed during a period when the success of the American revolution depended on it. Such is not the case today.

If the right to bear arms were absolute, people could carry guns into grocery stores and banks. Children could take guns with them to school. Our society decided long ago that it is in the best interests of society to place limits on gun ownership and the use of guns. In so doing, we rejected a literal interpretation of the Constitution. Those who favor stricter gun control laws should not be portrayed as wanting to deny the Constitution. They simply want to draw the line at a different place. In the 1770s, guns were necessary to defend this country. In the 1990s, guns are destroying it.

POINTS OF UNITY

Christians should be able to affirm that people are morally responsible for the choices they make. We should also affirm that difficult circumstances can have a major influence on those choices. We should be at least as interested in helping people make good choices as we are in punishing them for bad choices. And we must not forget that all human beings, no matter who they are or what they have done, bear God's image.

Chapter Thirteen

Homosexuality, Racism, the Media, the Environment, and Foreign Policy

---

The fact that we have grouped these five topics in one chapter does not mean they are less significant than other issues. In fact, we regard as important all of the issues we have chosen to address. We have touched on each of the five issues listed above— some more than others—in previous chapters. Yet because of their high visibility and importance, we deemed that each merited at least some individual treatment.

Again, we are aware of the impossibility of treating any of these issues thoroughly in five pages or less. But, as stated in the introduction to Part 2 of this book, our purpose is to illustrate moderate principles for the political debate, to provide food for thought as opposed to conclusive analysis. Even though our treatment of the issues below is less extensive, we continue our practice of introducing most topics with a quotation from someone widely respected by the Religious Right.

HOMOSEXUALITY

I have found myself consciously, in the last several years, avoiding just plain old-fashioned gay bashing. In the first place, it is unchristian, and in the second place, it just doesn't work. It doesn't persuade anybody.

William F. Buckley in response to a question about the rhetoric of the Religious Right[1]

Perhaps the most common phrase Christians hear—and repeat—in relation to the issue of homosexuality is the admonition to "love the sinner, but hate the sin." Everyone knows this is what they are supposed to do. But we struggle—as individuals and as a broader community of believers—over where tolerance and understanding ought to end and judgment ought to begin.

For example, many evangelicals have mixed feelings as they consider a biblical response to AIDS, which, though not an exclusively "gay disease," has become a proxy issue for the larger debate on homosexuality. A commitment to unconditional compassion for AIDS victims is mediated by a concern for public and private morality, particularly as it relates to drug abuse and illicit sexual behavior. The agenda of pro-gay radicals, after all, goes far beyond AIDS. Ultimately, that agenda calls for "sexual preference" to be beyond moral judgment. It calls for redefining the family through legislation that legally recognizes "domestic partners" and grants tax and insurance benefits that accompany such recognition.

At the other ideological extreme are the Christian Reconstructionists, who, in accordance with their version of theocracy, believe that self-avowed and practicing homosexuals should be stoned to death. While not going that far, other conservatives favor public policies that curtail civil rights of homosexuals, including the right to serve in the military.

Moderate evangelicals who have attempted to find middle ground have experienced the wrath of extremists on both sides of the ideological fence. John Huffman, Jr., pastor of Newport Beach

(California) Presbyterian Church, is considered "homophobic" by pro-gay forces within the Presbyterian Church (USA) because he opposes the ordination of homosexuals. He has been criticized by conservatives, however, for allowing practicing homosexuals to join the church.[2]

After Pastor Ed Dobson, cofounder of Moral Majority and pastor of Calvary Church in Grand Rapids, Michigan, announced the church's policy of welcoming AIDS victims to its worship services, he got letters from people accusing him of being a "homo lover" and claiming the church would be overrun with homosexuals.[3]

The issue of homosexuality—and what the Bible says about it—is a perennial topic of debate in mainline churches. Pro-gay forces in the United Methodist, Presbyterian, Episcopal, and other mainline denominations maintain that their churches will one day change their minds on this issue, just as they did on the issue of women's ordination.

As evangelical moderates, we reject the argument that these two issues are related. The overwhelming majority of evangelical scholars who favor women's ordination oppose the ordination of homosexuals. Thomas E. Schmidt is among the evangelical scholars who have addressed the issue of homosexuality. In his book *Straight and Narrow?* he addresses in detail the arguments of revisionist scholars who maintain that the biblical passages traditionally used to oppose homosexuality have been misunderstood. Schmidt concludes that the "Genesis creation story provides the primary basis for a biblical perspective on sexuality, and both Jesus and Paul quote Genesis to support their affirmation of marriage as a permanent union between husband and wife."[4] At another point he writes, "Homosexual acts, according to Romans 1:26–27 (and supported by several other biblical passages), depart from the only acceptable avenue for the full expression of sexuality, which is heterosexual marriage."[5]

We recognize that not all Christians who are homosexuals accept the conclusions of Schmidt and other conservative scholars on this issue. We appeal to such persons to realize that reaching the sincere conclusion that homosexual practice is immoral should not be considered hateful, especially if those conclusions were reached with an open mind.

We support the policy at Huffman's church that welcomes homosexual persons but prohibits practicing homosexuals from holding positions of leadership. We believe this policy communicates the right message on this issue.

While we encourage Christians to support efforts to raise awareness of, and search for a cure for, AIDS, we reject the argument that failure to do so constitutes anti-gay bigotry. Some churches will choose other priorities. After all, AIDS is not the only tragic and deadly disease for which we have no cure, and already more is spent on AIDS research than on, for example, cancer research.[6] All moral judgments aside, the fact that AIDS is to a large extent preventable suggests that other deadly diseases should be given at least as much priority.

Homosexuals As Persons

While we support the church's traditional view that homosexuality is immoral, we reject the notion that in God's economy homosexual sins are somehow less acceptable than other sins. Christian leaders who repent of adultery are typically restored to positions of authority and leadership within a few years. It is hard to imagine this happening were those same persons to confess to homosexual sin.

A conscious effort to uphold the personhood of homosexuals goes a long way toward fulfilling the admonition to "love the sinner." In part, this entails resisting the temptation to define homosexuals exclusively in terms of their sexual preference. A person is not just a homosexual. He or she is also a teacher, a musician, a scholar, or a writer.

Film critic Michael Medved, a friend of conservatives, states, "The gay men and lesbian women who play prominent roles in the entertainment industry are as diverse and dissimilar as their straight colleagues. They are involved on every side of every significant issue that currently divides the popular culture. While some of them certainly turn out work that denigrates traditional values and glorifies ugliness, others create wholesome entertainment that Middle America embraces with grateful enthusiasm."[7]

Says John Huffman, "I know I have been enriched by gay and lesbian persons. I have found that homosexual persons tend to bring to the church gifts of sensitivity, spiritual awareness, and creativity."[8] Perhaps homosexual persons who are involved with the church are more sensitive because of their painful struggles to understand themselves and their confusing desires, desires that are despised by both church and society. Schmidt writes, "These are people with faces, people with names, often Christian people, and whatever we conclude about the larger issues their stories represent, we must never lose sight of their individual struggles, their individual pain, their faces. If we neglect faces, we neglect the gospel."[9]

Upholding the personhood of homosexuals entails a compassionate effort to identify with their struggles and temptations. Some Christians want to dismiss as irrelevant the question of how people become homosexuals. How can we know how to help homosexual persons without knowing the answer to this question?

Ideologues on both sides of this debate have trouble admitting that in 1996 we simply do not know with certainty why some people have a homosexual orientation. Some evidence suggests a genetic determinant. Others have cited experiences of childhood and youth, particularly a deficit in the relationship with the same-sex parent. Former Olympic champion diver Greg Louganis, who is homosexual, writes, "Dad wasn't the type of father who would give you a hug and say that he loved you. He was stoic and, except for anger, not very good at expressing his emotions.... The best way to deal with Dad was to steer clear. It was like we were on eggshells at home because of Dad, and even then, he'd fly off the handle, especially when he was drinking, and he drank every night."[10] We urge people on both sides of this issue not to dismiss out of hand evidence that challenges their position.

We also encourage churches to recognize ministry to homosexuals and AIDS victims as a legitimate and much-needed option. Not only does such ministry embody God's unconditional love for all people, but it testifies to a church that is more willing to engage the world at its points of need than to retreat into familiar cloisters of piety.

Finally, in matters of public policy, we distinguish between private behavior and public policies that have the effect of advancing what we consider immorality. As moderates, we urge believers to oppose the efforts of the radical gay movement to influence policies related to taxes, insurance benefits, and families based on the contention that sexual orientation is as amoral as left-handedness. We believe public policies should provide incentives—financial or otherwise—that encourage moral behavior.

Nevertheless, we oppose efforts to deny homosexuals fundamental civil rights, including the right to live and work where they choose to live and work. While we support the rights of Christian organizations to discriminate based on sexual orientation, we believe that government must not do the same. Thus, we maintain that homosexuals who are willing to abide by the same regulations as others ought to be allowed to serve in the military.

We expect that many conservatives will attack us for taking this stand. We ask only that they do so in light of Ray Bakke's observation that "the Israelis, Germans and Canadians ... openly permit gays and lesbians in the military" and that "all have disciplined militaries." He continues, "I'm interested that while so many Americans are pro-Israel, they seem unaware that Israel pioneered the modern use of women and gays in military life."[11]

RACISM

> I have to ask, much to our shame, "Where were the white churches
> speaking out for what was right in those days?"
>
> Lieutenant Governor Mike Huckabee of Arkansas at the Christian Coalition's 1995 Road to
> Victory conference, addressing the silence of white Christians during the civil rights movement

According to one definition, racism is the belief that one race is innately superior to another. In the context of America, the superior race is usually white, though we must not fail to recognize the presence of a black supremacy movement. We maintain that the overwhelming majority of Christians in this country, including those who are part of the Christian Right, reject the view that the white race is superior. One of the Religious Right's most inspiring and beloved spokespersons is African-American Alan Keyes. And for years, Ben Kinchlow has been a close friend and associate of Pat Robertson on *The 700 Club*.

Only recently, however, has the conservative church begun to acknowledge and repent of its racist past. In 1995 the Southern Baptist Convention officially repented of its racist policies and attitudes. Also, the National Association of Evangelicals acknowledged last year failures in its dealings with black evangelicals. As moderates, we question whether the issue of racism occupies as high a place on the agenda of either political party or of the Christian Right as it ought to occupy.

During a discussion in the spring of 1995, one of the authors' more conservative friends expressed the view that black supremacist groups constituted a greater threat to the nation than white supremacist organizations. Less than a week later came the Oklahoma City bombing. At this writing, the extent of the connections between the accused bomber and white supremacist groups is uncertain. Yet through the incident, we received an eye-opening education about the size and organization of this country's white supremacist movement.

What if a black supremacy movement were equally well-armed

and organized? Not only would the nation, including the "liberal media," be concerned, but it would be alarmed and terrified. Doing something about the black supremacy movement would inevitably be on the political agenda of conservatives such as Pat Buchanan in a way that doing something about white supremacy is not.

Passive Racism

We do not want to downplay the genuine conversion that has taken place among religious conservatives over the last few decades with regard to issues of race. Many have acknowledged and repented of their views of white racial superiority. Because of that, conscious racism has largely diminished in the conservative Christian community. However, we challenge conservatives to move beyond a simplistic definition of racism in order better to understand its insidious nature and the varied forms it takes.

This means affirming the reality of a category called passive racism, a category that encompasses expressions of racial insensitivity. Some in the past have called it "benign" racism, but that label is itself racist in that it considers the "benignity" of racism only from the perspective of the offender. While no harm may be intended, the person who is victimized nevertheless feels demeaned. From the perspective of the victim, there is no such thing as harmless, "benign" racism.

Examples of unintentional racism abound in our culture, including the Christian culture. Ralph Reed devotes a chapter in his book, *Politically Incorrect,* to opposing racism. Yet at another point in the book, he states that each historical age can be summarized in a sentence. He calls the sixteenth century the "'age of discovery,' a time when the sails of European explorers dotted the oceans in pursuit of the New World, where they discovered gold, silver, and wealth beyond the wildest imaginations." He calls the eighteenth century the "age of revolution, as political turmoil convulsed Europe, and a bloody war in America tore the colonies from Great Britain."[12]

No doubt, neither Reed nor his editors realized how this capsule history might hurt and offend African-American and Native American readers. From a Native American perspective, the sixteenth century was the age of annihilation. From a black perspective, the seventeenth through the nineteenth centuries constituted the age of dehumanization. Reed's account typifies the approach of the overwhelming majority of white scholars and historians, who view past and present only from the perspective of white Europeans. As Hispanic historian Justo Gonzalez puts it, "History is written by the winners."

In fairness to Reed, his historical overview is offered in passing. It is not intended to be the major point in this section of his book. But it is precisely in such an unthinking environment where racial insensitivity, passive racism if you will, thrives.

In the authors' judgment, the institutions of a predominantly white evangelical subculture, including its publications and media ministries, are guilty of varying degrees of racial insensitivity. By and large, the kinds of issues and priorities these institutions address are issues of the white middle class. For example, our conversations with black Christian leaders suggest they are thankful for Focus on the Family's positions on moral issues, but are at odds with Focus's positions on various social and public policy issues, positions that often militate against what they are trying to accomplish in urban areas.

Those who attempt to call attention to subtle expressions of racism are typically dismissed by conservatives as being "politically correct." That might explain why conservatives for the most part refuse to use the term "African-American," even though that is what many African-Americans prefer to be called. We suspect that these same conservatives, who now hail Martin Luther King as a hero, three decades ago would have considered him "politically correct," too, had the term been in vogue.

Racism's Insidious Character

It is one thing to repent of past racism and quite another thing to acknowledge and address the effects that remain with us today. A television news feature a few years ago illustrates the insidious nature of racism. A hidden camera established that cab drivers are less likely to stop to pick up a black person than to pick up a white person. This was the case not only for white cab drivers, but for blacks as well. Some whites will look at that and conclude that it must not be racism if black cabbies are doing it to their own people.

An alternative conclusion, however, is that the evils of racism are such that it has succeeded in penetrating not only white culture, but African-American culture, too. That blacks have learned to despise and mistrust one another may very well be the most tragic consequence of white racism in America. Nathan McCall has argued that the phenomenon of black-on-black crime is really a form of self-hatred. The culture has taught black people to despise themselves and they take out their hatred on their own kind because they constitute an extension of self.[13]

Racism's effects remain with us also in the form of institutional racism, the nature of which is well illustrated by an anecdote from the long-running news program *Nightline*. Fill-in host Chris Wallace was grilling a representative of a private golf club that had no black members, despite nondiscriminatory policies. Wallace's guest claimed that neither he nor other club members held racist views. He explained simply that no black persons had ever applied for membership.

Wallace suggested that the golf club should make it a top priority to enlist a black member if for no other reason than to deflect the charges of racism. The guest might well have given the same advice to Wallace by suggesting that his network deflect allegations of racial bias by taking on a black news anchor.

The reality is that if all personal feelings of racism were to vanish suddenly, the legacy of this country's historical racism would still permeate our social and cultural institutions. African-Americans are not well represented at the local country club or on the PGA tour because golf is a rich person's game and historically African-Americans have not had fair access to the wealth and social privileges prerequisite to recreational golf.

An analysis of institutional racism must address the question of how people have arrived at places of privilege and influence in society's cultural and business institutions. Talent and the willingness to work hard certainly have something to do with it. But no honest assessment can ignore the truth of the adage, "It's not what you know, it's who you know."

Acknowledging the reality of institutional racism is far easier than addressing it. Sincere Christians who would subscribe to the analysis above nevertheless differ with respect to political solutions to the problem. The solution is more complicated than replacing rich white people with rich black people.

Until recently, the nation has attempted to repair inequities of the past through affirmative action programs. Opponents say affirmative action militates against African-Americans taking responsibility and feeds the perception that blacks do not deserve what they get. Advocates cite the new black middle class as evidence of the thousands who have benefited from affirmative action.

Not all African-Americans support affirmative action; not all white people oppose it. There is no reason why people on both sides of this issue cannot discuss it within a context of friendship and mutual respect. Both sides ought to concede, however, that the problems affirmative action was intended to address are still with us abundantly.

Some contend that institutional racism has affected biblical scholarship. In his book *Troubling Biblical Waters,* biblical scholar Cain Hope Felder makes a compelling case alleging the "total inadequacy and racial bias of the West's intellectual tradition in its efforts to provide allegedly *universal* conceptual and religious norms."[14] He adds that "much of Eurocentric scholarship, particularly in the last two centuries, readily takes offense at any suggestion that the Bible reflects a strong and favorable ancient Black presence."[15] We do not suggest that Felder and others plowing new ground in the name of Afrocentrism are right on all counts, but their ideas and theories deserve serious consideration.

A Word to the Left

In addition to our challenge to the Right, we have suggestions to people on the political Left aimed at enhancing dialogue among the races. For one thing, some define racism in terms of the majority culture's de facto privileged status, as well as its suppression—at personal, cultural, and institutional levels—of minorities. This understanding of racism tends to suggest that a white person is racist simply by virtue of being white. It further suggests that racism exclusively inhabits the domain of the majority culture, rendering the concept of "reverse racism," by definition, an oxymoron. Such a model has little or no space to address unhealthy attitudes that minority persons hold toward whites.

Those on the Left would do well to remember that racism is not the only "ism" that thrives in the land. Every day in this country people are unfairly judged based on physical size and beauty or on physical or mental ability. Some sociologists have argued that much of what is commonly considered race-related discrimination actually owes more to class than race. Certainly O. J. Simpson's class was a bigger factor than his race in his ability to secure a fair trial.

It is true that employers make judgments based in part on job candidates' abilities to use the English language, both in speech and in writing. In effect this means that African-Americans must in many cases learn to talk like whites. But the same is true for white people from the Deep South or rural America who must also make a cultural adjustment in order to succeed. One of the arguments against affirmative action is that it wrongly presumes that all black people grew up enjoying fewer privileges than all white people. This effectively elevates concerns about racism to a higher status than concerns about classism.

Even for some in the African-American community, racism is not the primary "ism." One does not have to look long or hard to find African-American women who feel called to pastoral ministry and who report that the barriers based on society's racism pale in comparison to the barriers of sexism they must face within their own black church communities.

As with those on the Right, we challenge those on the Left to distinguish between active and passive racism. It is counterproductive to hurl the invective "racist" at those whose insensitivity is based on ignorance. White people who are trying to "get it right" are understandably offended, hurt, and confused to be called "racist," a term that lumps them into the same category as white supremacists.

White people are not alone but are joined by African-American people who are sometimes hurt and offended by the rhetoric emanating from some politically liberal African-Americans who define black identity in terms of political viewpoints. One well known black pastor in a public lecture made a comic reference to the NAACP: the National Association for the Advancement of "Clarencized" People.[16] His obvious intent was to imply that Clarence Thomas and other politically conservative blacks have sacrificed their black identity by opting for politically conservative views. We regard this as arrogant.

We share Carl Ellis's view that in some segments of the black community, African ethnicity has wrongly become "the highest reference point."[17] States Ellis, an African-American pastor, "This is idolatry and Christians should never buy into it." Ellis adds that there is absolutely nothing wrong with celebrating Afrocentric heritage, manifested in personal preferences in clothing, art, music, and worship. But ultimately "African ethnicity [is] subject to a higher truth."[18]

Finally, we caution against the tendency instinctively to blame racism for all the problems of the black community. According to African-American writer Stanley Crouch, there was "no community, regardless of class, in the middle '50s that was any more ... devoted to the richest conception of civilization than the Afro-American community."[19] Crouch believes that many of the problems of the black community have arisen from within. He condemns rap music for celebrating anarchy and encouraging immorality. He says, "If those Rap videos and lyrics were written by a group of white people who were constantly depicting young black teenagers as sluts and hostile, murdering, trivial brutes who

... do nothing but smoke fat reefers and drink 40-ounce bottles of beer and walk around looking like clowns, the civil rights organizations would have been lined up outside the studio years ago."[20]

Getting to Know You

The gulf between the races is widened by the reality that black people and white people, for the most part, still live in different neighborhoods, work in different offices, and worship in different churches. We barely know each other, though blacks by necessity are far more familiar with the majority culture than most whites are with African-American culture.

We challenge Christians—black and white—to get to know one another better on a personal and social level. We need more integrated communities, workplaces, churches, and social lives. One of the greatest contributions of sports to American society has been to illustrate that for people who are working together as a team in pursuit of a common goal, skin color becomes a non-issue.

If we are to become more genuinely integrated, we believe the white community, especially Christians, must take the initiative in light of the residual feelings of insecurity, if not inferiority, in the African-American community at large. From the vantage point of those of us who are white, the problem of racism takes on a greater sense of urgency when people we care about have experienced it personally. Among the authors' friends are a man who has lived with the childhood memory of his uncle being hanged by a lynch mob in the 1950s. Another is an African-American woman who was working at the respected Catholic University in the 1990s when someone told her that her viewpoints were unimportant because she was "a nigger." Two more—a white pastor and his wife from a small All-American city in Pennsylvania—have experienced in the 1990s harassment from the Ku Klux Klan because of their three adopted interracial children.

Racism becomes more than another debatable issue as we get to know and care for people who have experienced its sting.

To the extent that we count these people as brothers, sisters, and friends, their pain, frustration, and righteous anger become our own.

THE MEDIA

> This year, a much more pervasive climate of sleaze has quietly descended over the early-evening hours.
>
> Jonathan Storm, in a 1995 *Philadelphia Inquirer* article on prime-time network television[21]

Someone trying to learn English from listening to Christian radio would walk away believing there is such a word as "liberalmedia." In conservative circles, the words "liberal" and "media" are as inseparable as C. S. Lewis and his pipe.

Most conservatives would never expect the "liberalmedia" to do an article criticizing network "sleaze," such as illicit sex and scatological humor. But the quotation leading off this topic is taken from a major metropolitan daily newspaper article titled "Off-color Television: Prime-time Shows Dirtying Up Their Act." This article was not buried in the entertainment section. It appeared—with a six-column headline—on the front page of the Sunday edition of the *Philadelphia Inquirer*. It's enough to cause cognitive dissonance in the minds of those convinced that the media are liberal beyond redemption.

Meanwhile, those on the other end of the political spectrum consider the media hopelessly conservative. Both political extremes sponsor media watchdog groups in the nation's Capitol that spend their time gathering evidence to support their conclusions about the media.

Determining who is right or wrong revolves around defining terms and establishing criteria: What exactly is meant by "liberal" and "conservative" in the context of the media? If we examine surveys that reveal how often media people go to church, how they vote, and what they think about issues such as abortion and homosexuality, the media would have to be considered liberal. According to a survey conducted by the Times Mirror Center for the People and the Press, only half as many national journalists as the general public attend church or synagogue regularly. Only 5 percent identify themselves as conservatives, while 22 percent say they are liberals and 39 percent consider themselves moderates.[22] While over half the general public believes that homosexuality should be discouraged, eight in 10 journalists, according to the survey, say it should be accepted.[23]

While conservatives, including Christians, are clearly under-represented in the ranks of the media, we should note that they are by no means absent. What's more, these surveys are usually limited to national journalists. Based on what we have observed, we suspect that television media people and print journalists who serve local audiences in cities around the country come closer to representing mainstream values.

In terms of the coverage of religion, it would be hard to argue that the media have been fair. According to a 1989 survey by the Religious News Service, readers would like newspapers to give religion higher priority than sports, entertainment, the arts, and personal advice.[24] Yet big city newspapers typically assign three or four reporters to cover one sports team and one person to cover the entire world of religion. Often that person is someone who has little knowledge of religion. Reporters who cover the business world are expected to have had some experience in business, whereas religious people are sometimes considered too biased to cover religion.

In some quarters, however, this trend has been reversed. *U.S. News and World Report* devotes several cover stories per year to religion-related issues. ABC News recently added a full-time religion reporter to contribute to its "American Agenda" segment. In a survey conducted by the First Amendment Center at Vanderbilt University, 72 percent of newspaper editors nationwide said that "religion is personally important to them."[25] And according to the Media Research Council, prime-time TV news and entertainment shows referred to religion twice as often in 1994 as in 1993. Those references were positive 44 percent of the time, compared with 23 percent negative.[26]

The Media: Liberal or Conservative?

Evaluating how liberal or conservative the media are depends partly on who is included in the evaluation. Certainly the major national media lean toward the ideological Left. But if we define the media in terms of all those who have access to the airwaves, the inclusion of such radio and television personalities as Pat Robertson, Pat Buchanan, Rush Limbaugh, William Buckley, James Dobson, and Jerry Falwell tips the scales toward the Right. In addition to his radio presence on thousands of stations nationwide, Dobson's syndicated newspaper column is represented in nearly 8 million American households. These conservative commentators have few equals on the Left.

If we examine the media's instinctive response to the Oklahoma City bombing, they would have to be considered Right-leaning. The media helped feed the speculation that the atrocity must have been committed by some terrorist from the Middle East, not a white American, especially someone with short hair and no facial hair who had served his country faithfully.

One might also ask, How could a liberal news magazine select Newt Gingrich as its Man of the Year, as *Time* did in 1995? Speaking of *Time*, one would be hard-pressed to find a more eloquent and forceful argument for sexual abstinence than is found in Lance Morrow's essay in the issue of October 2, 1995.

Those on the Left maintain that when it comes to coverage of foreign issues, the media cover the issues from the perspective of U.S. interests, as opposed to being objective. During the Gulf War, for example, information released by the Defense Department favorable to the United States was reported by the media as fact, even though much of it was later established as untrue or misleading.

Many conservatives accused the media of covering Bill Clinton more favorably than George Bush during the 1992 election season. But according to the Times Mirror Center survey, two-thirds of the American public felt Clinton's character problems were overplayed by the media. The media also made a big issue of Clinton's $200 haircut and have covered "Whitewatergate" far more aggressively than they covered George Bush's association with the Iran-Contra scandal.

The fact remains that people will find in the media whatever bias they are looking for. So instead of instinctively calling the media "liberal" on the one hand or "establishment" on the other for reasons of political expedience, we urge those on both sides to be specific with their charges.

The media's inherent deficiencies are sometimes wrongly mistaken for political bias. The very words "the media" bring to mind a nameless, faceless monster. In fact, journalists are people, including Christian people, with names and faces. They have limitations. Sometimes they are asked to become "experts" on a particular issue or situation literally overnight or to reduce complex topics to short, readable paragraphs under the pressure of deadlines. A baseball player can fail to get a hit in two out of three trips to the plate and still go to the Hall of Fame. Not so with reporters. Journalists who fall short should be corrected, but we should not jump to the conclusion that inaccuracies or misrepresentations constitute intentional bias. Christians who have taken the time to build relationships with the local and national press are usually rewarded with more responsible and friendlier coverage.

The Entertainment Media

People will also find whatever bias they are looking for in the entertainment media, as the American Life Lobby proved in 1995 by revealing that a child had noticed the word "sex" spelled out in the stars in a scene from the animated movie *The Lion King*. This had somehow eluded the eyes of millions of other viewers.

As with evaluating the news media, any objective evaluation of the entertainment media, especially television, leads to mixed conclusions. The *Philadelphia Inquirer* article cited above raised many valid points. Among them is the observation that, in response to viewer research, network television has given up on children and older viewers and is focusing instead on the 18–49 age range. According to the article, the way to do that is "to make shows that bristle with sexual situations and provocative language."[27]

These concerns notwithstanding, the news from the network television front is not all bad. Such shows as *Home Improvement, Step by Step,* and *Sister, Sister* uphold traditional values. *Touched by an Angel* is an hour-long religious sermon. The issue of abortion is rarely addressed on network television. Homosexuals are portrayed favorably sometimes, but they are also stereotyped and stigmatized. Religion is treated simplistically or not at all. Sometimes fundamentalists are treated as buffoons, but so are animal rights activists.

This is not to deny, but merely to qualify, the concerns of conservatives. After all, we too are alarmed that during the spring of the 1991 "sweeps" period, according to media critic Michael Medved, the American Family Association "logged a total of 615 instances of sexual activity depicted or discussed on prime-time shows" and that by "a margin of *thirteen to one* (571 to 44) these references favored sex outside marriage over intimate relations between life partners."[28]

Given conservatives' concerns about what the free market has produced in terms of network television fare, we find it immensely ironic that the Christian Right opposes government funding of public television, much of which is constituted by values-neutral educational fare. Certainly there are some things on public television that conservatives find objectionable, but it also provides a home base for such renowned conservatives as William Buckley. It is the height of irony that conservatives want to eliminate government support of public television, which last year gave Barbara Dafoe Whitehead a platform from which to tell the world that Dan Quayle was right about traditional family values.[29]

Even the worst of network television pales in comparison to what Hollywood is providing these days. Although much of his analysis is one-sided, Michael Medved, in his 1992 book *Hollywood vs. America,* raised many valid concerns regarding the movie industry's biases against religion, the family, and traditional moral values. Without down-playing the importance of those concerns, we offer the following qualifications.

First, while Hollywood is not exactly a nesting place for Christian virtue, neither is it everything that some of those on the ideological Left would like it to be. Michael Medved acknowledges that pro-gay activists exert considerable influence on the entertainment industry. But taking issue with some conservatives, he writes, "Those who look for evidence of some huge 'gay conspiracy' at the heart of Hollywood will be frustrated in that search, for the simple reason that no such conspiracy exists."[30] He adds, "For every motion picture that offers an approving view of a gay character, it's easy to find one that emphasizes negative stereotypes— portraying homosexuals as crazed killers or swishy objects of ridicule."[31] Certainly, some stars may wear their red ribbons on Oscar night in support of the homosexual community, but when they make movies, it's still Aladdin running off with Jasmine, the little mermaid with Prince Eric, and Meg Ryan with whoever happens to be the lucky guy.

Second, conservatives are correct in calling attention to gratuitous sex and violence. In evaluating art, however, it would behoove us all to distinguish between superfluous or unnecessary violence, sex, and language and that which is functional to the telling of the story. Many true and important stories that help us gain insight into the human condition cannot be told without descriptions of pathology. If the only standards were sex and violence, the Bible itself would be off limits.

Another pitfall of this narrow focus is the automatic assumption that any movie free of undue sex and violence is automatically good. For example, movie critic Ted Baehr gives us a thumbs up to Disney's *Lion King*. Baehr does not call attention to what some regard as the movie's implicit naturalistic worldview. This is not to say that *The Lion King* is a bad movie. In fact, we believe it affirms important values and is highly entertaining. Yet Christian parents should at least be aware of the full range of messages that it may be communicating to their children.

The fundamental problem is that so few motion pictures operate from a Christian worldview. In fact, some films are anti-Christian. In a pluralistic society, we should not expect all motion pictures to function as two-hour-long gospel tracts, but we can express dismay that Christian values and a Christian worldview are largely absent.

Third, the absence of Christian values is attributable in part to the retreat mentality that has led Christians to abandon the entertainment industry. As a community, when things haven't gone our way, we have been too quick to "take our ball and run home," instead of getting into the mix and trying to change things. However, many believers who are active in Hollywood have found open doors and opportunities for Christians to make a positive difference.

Common Ground

Conservatives and liberals might find some common ground in calling attention to media-related concerns that have nothing to do with ideological divisions. Among these is the media's tendency to insult human sensitivities in order to increase ratings or to fulfill the public's right to know. Said one psychologist who helped counsel victims' families after the Oklahoma City bombing, "In our media-driven culture, we must help victims and survivors exercise the right to say, 'I need to be left alone right now. If you follow me you are being unkind.' Many reporters welcomed the boundaries that we set in Oklahoma City, and said privately that it dignified their efforts, giving them an answer for editors who were pressuring them to behave more aggressively."

Christians should continue to challenge and influence the media with respect to their responsibility not just to report on our culture but to shape culture in positive ways. In that regard, we should all be able to agree that *Time*'s decision, as part of its reporting on the Japanese subway gas bomb attack in 1995, to inform its readers in graphic detail about how easy it is to make deadly weapons was simply irresponsible.

Conservatives and liberals alike should be concerned with the trend toward sensationalism on the part of the media. This reached its apex with coverage of the O. J. Simpson trial. Our culture's voyeuristic tendencies inspired some media outlets to adopt an "all-O. J." format, and the market bore it with ease.

Even highly respectable news organizations have been influenced to varying degrees by the demand for sizzle over substance. The tendency toward the kind of "journalism" that exploits male hormones and other prurient interests is part of the price we pay for our commitment to a free market. For the hard reality is that all those O. J.-obsessed millions who need to get a life of their own are also consumers. News organizations are ultimately businesses that cannot achieve any lofty goals if they can't stay afloat. Even Pat Robertson, who supports family values in the entertainment media, declined the opportunity to give *Christy* a chance on the Family Channel because he was not sure it could make money.[32]

The media are ultimately businesses that people can choose to support or reject. And free people in democratic, capitalist America have spoken. In an era in which reputable and insightful news shows such as *The News Hour with Jim Lehrer* struggle to survive, the *National Enquirer* sells 3.5 million copies each week. If successful democracy depends on an informed electorate, the world's largest democracy could be headed for trouble.

As moderates, we believe that in this current media climate, government-funded public television has a vital and proper role to play in offering an alternative to journalistic and entertainment media that are exclusively market-driven. We believe that government is well within its rights to grant official support to educational television and the arts. Currently that support stands at less than five-hundreths of one percent. Some 84 percent of Americans believe funding for the Public Broadcasting System should be maintained or increased, while 79 percent of Republicans believe PBS programming "is neither too conservative nor too liberal."[33] We agree with the majority.

In this pluralistic society, people will inevitably disagree over what constitutes art. Conservatives' ire over some of what has passed as art is legitimate. But according to *Time* art critic Robert Hughes, of the "tens of thousands of grants that the [National Endowment for the Arts] has made in its 30-year history, perhaps a dozen have excited some serious controversy and only two . . . have brought it to the verge of abolition."[34] Those two are Robert Mapplethorpe's grotesque, homoerotic photo exhibit and Andres Serrano's photo of a crucifix in urine. And in both cases, the "artists" received no direct funding from the NEA.

All citizens, including Christians, have every right and responsibility to protest displays of art they find offensive, just as they have a right to speak out about objectionable military action on the part of the United States, which is also funded by their tax dollars. But given our assessment of the current high quality of public radio and television programming and the importance of artistic expression in the development of a culture, we believe the nation stands to lose far more from scrapping government funding of public television and the arts than from allowing occasional expressions of art that many consider offensive to slip through.

THE ENVIRONMENT

> We are to exercise dominion over [the things of nature] not as though entitled to exploit them, but as things borrowed or held in trust, which we are to use realizing that they are not our intrinsically.
>
> Francis Schaeffer[35]

Environmental care is almost totally absent from the Christian Right's agenda. In his book *Politically Incorrect*, Ralph Reed mentions environmentalism only in reference to the agenda of the Left. The environment was addressed in a workshop at the Christian Coalition's 1995 annual conference, but the focus was exclusively on government efforts to take away individual liberties in the name of environmental care.

It stands to reason that many conservative Christians' views of the end times have contributed to apathy with regard to the environment. After all, people who are convinced that Jesus is coming back soon believe there is no reason to care about conditions on earth 50 or 100 years from now. In addition, many conservatives are skeptical of what they consider to be alarmist claims of secular scholars such as Carl Sagan.

What the Bible says about care for creation is territory that theologians through the years have for the most part left unexplored, though Jacques Ellul, Karl Barth, and Francis Schaeffer are among those who stand out as exceptions to the norm. Some evangelical theologians operate out of a framework according to which the world, prior to the Fall, represents God's ideal. Those scholars who subscribe to a theology according to which God's plan from the beginning is to get us back to the world before the Fall would do well to note that in the world before the Fall, human beings were to eat only plants, not animals.[36]

In Genesis 1 the Hebrew phrase *nephesh chaya* is used in reference both to humans and to animals. The word is usually translated "living creatures" in reference to animals, but "living souls" or "living beings" with respect to humankind. This results in the perception of a greater distinction between animals and humans than the biblical text justifies.

After each stage of creation, God pronounced his creative work as being "good." Then God created human beings in his image and pronounced all of creation "very good." Herman Daly and John Cobb contend, "Translated into philosophical terms, this means that all creatures have intrinsic value, and that the addition of the human species gives to the whole a special excellence. Existence in general, and especially life, are to be affirmed in themselves, not merely in relation to ends that transcend them."[37]

The authors affirm that since "human beings are not merely one species among others," but are "specifically authorized to have dominion over the earth," to some extent, plant and animal life "function as means to human ends."[38] According to the authors, however, the "right of human beings to use [plants and animals] does not supersede their right to a place in the world."[39]

We believe the Bible teaches that human beings owe a deeper respect to nonhuman creation than they are currently offering. Were the late theologian Karl Barth alive today, he would no doubt be seriously disturbed that in our consumer society, some animals have no purpose on earth except to be treated as food commodities sold at 79 cents a pound. Mankind's "lordship over the living beast" takes on a

> new gravity when he sees himself compelled to express his lordship by depriving it of its life. He obviously cannot do this except under the pressure of necessity. Far less than all the other things which he dares to do in relation to animals, may this be ventured unthinkingly and as though it were self-evident.[40]

We find Rush Limbaugh's attitude—"If the owl can't adapt to the superiority of humans," tough luck![41]—to be incompatible with biblical principles.

We believe that having to choose between caring for the earth or caring for humanity is a false dichotomy. If the earth's problems are as serious as many scientists say they are, then not only are the land and water in for bad news, but so are people. Conservatives ought to realize that while many Christian scientists' theological beliefs are essentially the same as Ralph Reed's, they are convinced that Carl Sagan is closer than Rush Limbaugh to the truth when it comes to an analysis of the environmental threats facing this planet.

To be sure, environmental scientists are divided on some issues. For example, whereas many contend that global warming is a problem, others argue that heat waves in recent years are part of weather patterns that have existed for centuries. It should be noted that greenhouse skeptic Robert Balling of Arizona State University recently conceded, "The world is warming and warming in part from [human] forces."[42]

Some economists have argued that overpopulation is not the environmental hazard some have portrayed it to be. They have pointed out that if all of the world's billions of people were divided into families of four and given about half an acre of land, they would all fit neatly into an area of land the size of Texas. But as Christian biologist Dave Unander observes, however, "We'd be in big trouble if we all flushed our toilets at the same time."[43] Unander correctly observes that human life entails more than having a decent-sized house and yard. If everyone lived in Texas, there would be no room for golf courses, school buildings, hiking trails, and grocery stores. Beyond that, this earth must also support untold billions of animals and plants who contribute in their own ways to the sustaining of human life. The environmental challenge as it relates to population entails such challenges as renewing the earth's supply of oxygen and clean water. The fact is that the scientific community, including Christian scientists, is virtually unanimous in its concern about the earth's ability to sustain human life if population levels continue to increase.

Scientists are largely united in their concern about holes in the ozone layer, caused primarily by chlorofluorocarbons (CFCs). Yet some segments of conservative Christendom seem to be in denial. In the book *Whatever Happened to the American Dream?* Larry Burkett denies that this is a problem. In doing so, according to Larry Schweiger of the Chesapeake Bay Foundation, Burkett "rejects the findings of hundreds of leading scientists from 119 different countries, including scientists from virtually every manufacturer of CFCs."[44] According to Schweiger, Burkett sides instead "with two unqualified people who have never published on this subject in any peer-reviewed journal. They alone suggest that the ozone hole is a hoax."[45]

We agree with conservatives that some federal regulations related to environmental care have been unreasonable and have occasionally trampled on individual liberties. Yet we caution people not to believe every horror story they hear, even if it is told by a member of Congress. In a speech against "regulatory overkill," Congressman Michael Balaris of Florida claimed on the floor of the House that the Drinking Water Act limits arsenic levels in drinking water to "no more than two to three parts per billion," while shrimp served in restaurants contain 30 parts per billion. The truth is that the Drinking Water Act limits arsenic levels to 50 parts per billion, not two or three. And according to the EPA, the kind of arsenic found in water is far more toxic than that found in shrimp.[46]

Entrepreneurs who have been able to turn environmental stewardship into profit-making ventures should be applauded and encouraged. It is naive, however, to believe that all environmental problems will be addressed by the free market. For example, among the environmental problems of greatest concern in the eastern United States is the pollution of Chesapeake Bay. This problem actually originates in the Susquehanna River, which begins in New York State, runs through Pennsylvania and into Maryland before draining into the Chesapeake. At points along the way, runoff from cow manure finds its way into the river, which increases the amount of algae in it. In turn, this has a negative effect on the millions of fish that return from the Atlantic Ocean to lay eggs in their native Chesapeake. As the fish population declines, those who make their living fishing the North Atlantic are placed at risk.

The bottom line is that a farmer from upstate New York and a fisherman from the coast of Maine—two decent human beings who will probably never meet each other—are nevertheless intimately connected by an environmental problem of which neither is aware. We believe it is within the scope of government's responsibility to address this kind of problem.

Conservation and sportsmen's groups alike have expressed concern that a deregulatory-minded Republican Congress will reverse years of environmental progress. Newspaper outdoors columnist Fen Montaigne writes that "if there's something outdoorsmen of all political persuasions can agree upon, it is this: The federally led cleanup of the environment over the last quarter-century has brought about impressive improvements. Our rivers are generally cleaner. Many coastal waters . . . look better than they have in decades. A host of endangered species, from bald eagles to grizzly bears to gray whales, are bouncing back. Waterfowl populations are at a 20-year high."[47]

Between the Extremes

Environmentally conscious Christians who stand between the ideological extremes must balance their concerns for earthkeeping with the acknowledgment of the priority of humankind. Yet this can lead to difficult decisions, as in cases where people's livelihoods depend on business enterprises, such as logging companies and steel mills that do damage to the environment. It is far easier for a scientist to assess potential environmental damage from a distance than to tell a father of four that he's out of a job.

Nevertheless, if that father is out of work because all the trees are gone or if his children develop cancer or emphysema from unregulated industry, what was really gained from short-term corporate profit based on a completely *laissez-faire* approach to business? Also, when people like Limbaugh speak up on behalf of the poor logger, keep in mind that that logger is making perhaps only a few hundred dollars even though he cuts down hundreds of thousands of dollars worth of trees. It is really wealthy business people who have the most to lose from environmental regulation of the logging industry.

So when difficult choices must be made, we should take steps to minimize the potential negative effects of our choices. Such steps might include planting a tree for every one we cut down or attempting to find other employment for those forced to sacrifice their livelihood for the sake of the environment.

Sometimes difficult choices revolve around preservation of an endangered species. Some environmentalists favor whatever measures are necessary, no matter how extreme, to preserve species. At the other extreme are those who regard losing a species about as seriously as they regard losing a golf ball in a lake.

A moderate viewpoint stops short of elevating the protection of a species to an absolute principle. However, we must acknowledge that each life form, from the smallest microbe to the largest mammal, plays a role in the ecosystem of which it is a part. Clearly, once a species is lost, its potential contributions to humankind are gone forever. As a matter of principle, we must recognize the tremendous risk we are taking when we allow species of any kind to become extinct without fully understanding how its absence might affect the environment.

In the absence of consensus on how serious our environmental problems are, we maintain that the safest course of action is to err on the side of those who say the problems are serious, especially when solutions they suggest have negligible effects on productivity and freedom.

FOREIGN POLICY

> Today there is no military threat to the security of the United States or to the democracies with which we have been allied in the last half-century.
>
> Jeane Kirkpatrick at the Christian Coalition's 1995
> Road to Victory conference

Defense seems to be the only area of spending that has escaped the new conservative Congress's budget ax. We find this bewildering, given the priority of addressing the federal deficit and given that the Cold War has long been won and there are no immediate military threats to the United States on the horizon. We agree with James Skillen of the Center for Public Justice when he says, "We are at a point in history where the kinds of battles the United States faces are not the kinds that require a push in defense spending."[48]

It would be one thing if conservatives' motivation for these increases was to bring peace and assure basic human rights in other parts of the world. Unfortunately, however, this emphasis on maintaining high levels of defense spending is accompanied by a trend toward provincialism and isolationism. This is reflected in part by Pat Buchanan's position, shared by many on the Right, that there are no circumstances under which U.S. troops ought to serve under United Nations authority.

U.S. foreign policy has increasingly come to be influenced by what is deemed best only for this nation. For Christians, foreign policy must be guided not just by what seems best for America, but by what is morally right.

This was the primary consideration behind President Bush's decision to send U.S. troops to Somalia. A supporter of this action, World Vision President Robert Seiple observed in a *Christianity Today* interview that U.S. motives in Somalia were "both clear and right." Said Seiple, "There was no oil there or warm-water ports. There was nothing but the humanitarian desire to stop famine and war that were essentially destroying 2,000 children every day."[49]

Unfortunately, that military effort was not popular back home. Said Seiple, "I sense in the U.S. an increasing mood of isolationism. From a Christian perspective, this is antikingdom." He adds, "It's tragic that the question of national interests is never asked in the context of the value we place on human life and dignity. I believe it is in our national interests to take a stand for the humanity and sanctity of life."[50]

The subtle assumption behind an isolationist posture is that the United States is morally superior to other nations. That assumption was tested by accusations that three U.S. servicemen last November raped a 12-year-old Japanese girl in Okinawa. We can only imagine the moral outrage in the United States if three Japanese soldiers were accused of raping an American girl.

Perhaps what is most chilling in terms of a moral evaluation of the United States was not the rape itself, but the aftermath. Of all the things he could have said about the incident, U.S. Admiral Robert Macke chose the following words: "I think it was absolutely stupid, I've said several times. For the price they paid to rent the car, they could have had a girl." This statement did not come from someone fresh out of basic training, but from a 35-year veteran who was in charge of all U.S. military operations in the Pacific. Especially in the light of such incidents as the Tailhook scandal, this statement suggests that moral shortcomings among those representing the United States overseas are endemic, ignored by superiors if not endorsed from on high. Certainly this ought to call into question the assessment held by some that the United States is a shining moral light among the nations.

The isolationist urge is also evident in a trend to cut back on humanitarian foreign aid. According to a survey conducted by the University of Maryland's Program on International Policy Attitudes, seven out of 10 citizens believe the United States spends too much on foreign aid. Two out of three said they wanted to cut foreign spending.[51]

Their responses, however, may have been based on false assumptions. On average, respondents to the survey believed that the United States spends a whopping 18 percent of its budget on foreign aid. In reality, the figure is only about 1 percent.

U.S. Senator Jesse Helms of North Carolina would like it to be even less than that, which is why he sponsored a bill aimed at abolishing the U.S. Agency for International Development.[52] Thirty-two evangelical organizations who are active in overseas ministries opposed the bill. As evangelical moderates, we side with them.

Christians must take the lead in developing foreign policy and must do so with biblical values at the forefront. We must seek answers to such questions as, How should our world be ordered? What form should its legal, political and economic institutions take? How can we best offer hope and help?

The answers will not be achieved incidentally or through technological progress. Order will come through the efforts of wise persons, people who are commited to working for truth and progress. When the world asks America, What are your truths?, we must be prepared to answer in ways that will bring peace to a world riddled with belligerence, justice to a world with manifold inequalities, and freedom to a world that is the scene of multiple enslavements, including religious persecution. The Bible defines sin partly in terms of what we don't do. To become isolationists is to abdicate our moral responsibility.

Chapter Fourteen

A Political Agenda for Evangelical Moderates

Most of the vision that people of faith have for a caring society cannot be achieved through political action.

Ralph Reed[1]

In a *Time* magazine cover story, Ralph Reed described the Christian Coalition as "the McDonald's of American politics." In response, a letter writer states, "What a perfect description. They both have a limited menu."[2] This assessment goes a long way toward capturing what we find wrong with the political approach of the Christian Right.

We respect Ralph Reed's intelligence, his abilities, and his commitment to do what he thinks is right for this country. We similarly respect all those on the Religious Right—leaders and followers—who have made major sacrifices of time, energy, and financial resources in an effort to make a positive difference. We wish more Christians with different political leanings would make a similar investment, in part so that the world could see more readily the political diversity within the community of believers. What's more, we agree with some of what the Religious Right stands for in terms of moral and social values. Again, our disagreement focuses primarily on how it represents itself and on what it does not say. The following is a summary of our political convictions:

We define abortion in terms of justice for the unborn, not in terms of reproductive choice. We believe that eliminating unwanted pregnancies should be a top national priority. We suspect that many on the Right agree. But we also affirm the full equality of women and their freedom to serve equally with men as leaders in the home, church, and society. And given that women are usually left to pick up the pieces of broken families, we call on tougher measures against deadbeat dads and urge political leadership to make a serious effort to curb the problem of domestic abuse.

We oppose, along with the Religious Right, public policies that presume that homosexual behavior is morally acceptable. But we call for defending the civil rights of homosexual persons, and we encourage all people to affirm that homosexuals, too, bear the image of God.

We maintain that government should support, rather than supplant, other social institutions, especially the family. We favor programs that do not give without expecting something in return. We support programs that help diffused and disconnected people, especially children, as opposed to special interest groups who have the power to lobby. We believe that government should focus on providing services not currently provided by the free market.

We support the rights of citizens to own guns both for purposes of recreation and self-defense. Most on the Right would agree. But we do not regard efforts to set limits on gun ownership as a threat to citizens' fundamental rights. We maintain that political leaders should seek the wisdom of those who have the most to lose—law enforcement officers and people in the inner city—from lax gun control laws. Taking their advice, we believe, would lead to far stricter requirements for gun ownership and to an outright ban on all assault weapons.

We support freedom for religious expression and the teaching of values in public schools, as does the Right. But we oppose requiring religious expression and we oppose measures that grant special privileges or visibility to a particular religion. Thus, we oppose government-sponsored prayer in schools, as well as the posting of the Ten Commandments. We support the concept of allowing students time off to receive values education in accordance with the religion of their choice.

We believe that parents, not government, bear ultimate responsibility for educating children. The authors disagree with one another on the related issues of educational vouchers and tuition tax credits, but we regard tax support for public education as a duty required of all citizens for the sake of the common good. Thus, educational vouchers, if they are applied, should serve only to give more choices to poorer families, not to give the wealthy a means to avoid paying school taxes.

We believe, along with the Religious Right, that schools should teach children the highest moral and political values that gave birth to and have sustained the great nation of the United States of America. We believe further that children should learn these values in ways that engender respect, love, and loyalty to this nation. The result of such education, however, should not be self-righteous pride and arrogance, but a heightened sense of responsibility to be a moral example to the world. This means that the moral failures of the United States—past and present—must not be denied or suppressed. It means that support for the United States should not be unconditional, nor should its actions and attitudes be beyond the critical moral judgment of the people.

We oppose racism as being both sinful and destructive to the productivity and morale of this nation. We challenge people, including those who identify with the Religious Right, to examine this insidious problem and its effects far more deeply and sincerely than they have done to date.

We believe that people are morally responsible for their actions and that if order is to be present in society, crime must be punished. But we would also attempt to bring greater consistency to the justice system, recognizing that justice unevenly administered is not justice at all. In addition, we support restitution, rehabilitation, and efforts at reconciliation between victim and offender. We advocate economic and political measures aimed at improving the quality of choices in our society, especially for those among whom crime is far too high on the list of options. And we believe that attempts to understand and address our culture's obsession with violence should become a top national priority both for the government and for the church.

We support efforts to reform the welfare system in ways that encourage personal responsibility and commitment to family. But we would be far more hesitant than many of those on the Right to differentiate conclusively between "deserving" and "undeserving" poor. We also maintain that the Right, in assessing this culture's morality, has largely ignored materialism and rampant individualism, neither of which can be reconciled with biblical admonitions toward community. We question whether the private sector would be able to fill the gaping holes that would be left by a rapid, ideologically motivated overhaul of the system. Thus, we would favor continued government oversight of the needs of the poor and the commitment on the part of government to look after those whom the private sector has failed to notice or help.

We maintain that faith-based charities that are attempting to address this country's social problems have been wrongly targeted for discrimination based on their religious character. We support a voucher system, which would enable those in need of social services to choose whichever organization or agency they think can help them the most, without regard to religious orientation.

We support efforts to ensure that the United States remains militarily strong. But in this time in which no significant threat to our national security exists—and in which the federal deficit is arguably our biggest national problem—we question the judgment of those who want to increase defense spending. We urge political leaders to hold the line on military spending and to resurrect talk about a "peace dividend." Furthermore, we uphold policies and attitudes that ensure that U.S. military strength is not based exclusively on selfish national interest. Taking issue with isolationists, we believe the United States has a moral obligation to uphold human rights in other parts of the world.

Upholding a Process

As has been mentioned repeatedly, however, the main purpose of this book is not to espouse "moderately correct" political positions. We have addressed issues primarily to illustrate their complexity and to show that Christians of similar faith can and do disagree politically. We have tried to demonstrate that on most issues today, as in the past, there are few clearly "Christian" positions.

Christians of goodwill disagree largely because they emphasize different biblical themes. For example, comparing those who have a well-developed theology of creation with those who stress a theology of the end times, the former group is more likely to make the environment a top priority. Of course, these emphases are not mutually exclusive. In the final analysis, we would encourage all Christians to develop a fuller, more complete theology.

We also encourage believers who differ politically to cooperate with one another on causes where they are of one mind. The theologically liberal National Council of Churches and the Christian Coalition both belong to the National Coalition Against Legalized Gambling.[3] Ron Sider of Evangelicals for Social Action serves on the board of directors of the San Diego-based environmental group Floresta along with Paul Thompson of Pat Robertson's organization Operation Blessing.

The political agenda we have sought to advance focuses mainly on a process heavily influenced by biblical values. This process grows out of the affirmation that Christians find their essential unity through their faith in Jesus Christ as Lord and Savior, not in their public policy positions.

We suspect that some of what we have written in this book will anger some conservatives, and perhaps others. But some conservatives have said and done things that have angered us as well. Being angry at one another, however, does not excuse us from pursuing unity. Psychologists, including Christian psychologists, tell us that some of the best marriages feature anger, albeit appropriately expressed. Learning how to fight fairly is good for a marriage. It acknowledges that no two people will always see eye-to-eye. And if two people who cared enough for each other to get married don't always agree, we can't expect this nation's tens of millions of evangelicals always to agree.

The track record among Christians over the past several centuries is far from glorious. Pelagius and Augustine conducted their mutually maligning fourth-century theological debate by mail. They never met one another. Clyde Manschreck informs us that in the 1500s, at the University of Tübingen, different schools of thought "were still vigorously advocated, and disputes often ended in fights with clubs and stones. Students lined up on the side of nominalism or realism, the two prevailing philosophies, and were assigned to their ... dormitories accordingly.... The disputes were often dangerous. Ludvicus Vives reported that he saw fighting not only with fists, but with clubs and swords, so that many were wounded and even killed."[4] We've come a long way since then. But we have further to go.

We live in difficult times. At last year's Christian Coalition conference Pat Robertson pointed out that for years the majority of Americans have been troubled with the direction in which this nation is heading. Whether Democrats or Republicans control Congress, surveys show the same results. This suggests that the fundamental problems that concern Americans are social and moral in nature. Developed and signed in 1995 by dozens of Christian leaders, the "Cry for Renewal" recognizes this as it calls churches "back to a biblical focus that transcends the Left and the Right."[5]

In times of trouble, ideologies become more attractive. They represent anchors in the storm, certainty amid the confusion. They bind people together who feel desolate and forsaken. They offer an escape from doubt and loneliness. They provide the easy answers that people need and seek. In contrast, broadening the agenda usually means listening to other people with different ideas and alternative political priorities. It introduces ambiguity and tentativeness into the equation.

For Christians, however, the goal is not political victory that provides a false sense of security. The goal is to do what is right. We cannot pretend there are easy political solutions to our nation's complex problems. If we do that—if we retreat to familiar and comfortable ideological ground—we will merely prevent ourselves from discovering genuine solutions that can make a real difference.

As evangelicals, we believe the ultimate solution is something agreed upon by Christians on the Left, on the Right, and at all points in between. That true solution is Jesus Christ. "Politics cannot solve our problems," claims the Cry for Renewal document. And almost all major speakers at the Christian Coalition's 1995 Road to Victory conference (not including Presidential candidates) echoed this theme in one form or another.

The church's capacity to proclaim Christ is severely limited when the political division is as bitter as it is today. As the Cry for Renewal puts it, "inflamed rhetoric and name calling is no substitute for real and prayerful dialogue between different constituencies with legitimate concerns and a gospel of love which can bring people together."

The church's witness to the world is harmed when followers of Jesus Christ place political loyalty on a higher plane than spiritual unity. Writing to the Romans, the apostle Paul does not suggest unity as an option, but sets it forth as a mandate. And that unity is found in Jesus Christ and in him alone.

We urge Christians to consider our "Ten Commandments of Moderate Political Behavior" as a model for striving toward unity and carrying on the conversation. In doing that, we must remember that we are brothers and sisters in Christ and that we are all part of a larger, world Christian family. That being the case, as we wrestle with one another on the issues, we have an obligation to do so honestly and fairly. Without denying that many issues are important to us, we must affirm that agreeing on political issues is not what brings us together in the first place. As long as we remember who unites us, our conversation will be guided by love, patience, longsuffering, openness, and integrity. Ultimately, biblical faith will triumph over mere ideology.

Let us never forget the awe-inspiring significance of our unity. Christians on the political Left and the political Right together affirm that the living God and Creator of all things came to earth in the person of Jesus Christ to die for the sins of humankind in order to reconcile the world to himself. By comparison, our divisions ought to seem less significant. If they don't, something is wrong with our priorities.

We believe it is incumbent upon Christian leaders across the political spectrum to find ways to express spiritual unity based on faith in Christ. Not only would this communicate something very important to the world, but it would constantly keep before us the church's greater mission, rather than a particular political agenda.

That greater mission is to proclaim the news that Jesus offers life. It is to encounter others at their points of need. It is to do what Jesus told us to do: visit prisoners, clothe the naked, and feed the poor. We do so motivated not by guilt but by grace; not because others deserve it, but because we don't deserve it either; not because we must, but because we can. In this way we model a future kingdom in which all political differences will pass away.

Bibliography

Achebe, Chinua. *Hopes and Impediments*. New York: Doubleday, 1989.

Almond, Gabriel Abraham, and Sidney Verba. *Civic Culture*. Princeton, NJ: Princeton University Press, 1963.

Arendt, Hannah. *On Revolution*. New York: Viking Press, 1965.

Bailyn, Bernard. *Ideological Origins of the American Revolution*. Cambridge: Harvard University Press, 1967.

Bane, Mary Jo, and David T. Ellwood. *Welfare Realities: From Rhetoric to Reform*. Cambridge: Harvard University Press, 1994.

Bellah, Robert. *Beyond Belief*. New York: Harper & Row, 1978.

____. *The Broken Covenant*. Chicago: University of Chicago Press, 1992.

____ *Habits of the Heart*. Berkeley: University of California Press, 1938.

Bellah, Robert, et al. *The Good Society*. New York: Knopf, 1991.

Berger, Peter L. *The Capitalist Revolution*. New York: Basic Books, 1986

____. *Facing up to Modernity*. New York: Basic Books, 1977.

Berman, Harold J. *The Interaction of Law and Religion*. Nashville: Abingdon Press, 1974.

Black, Hugo. *A Constitutional Faith*. New York: Knopf, 1967.

Bloom, Allan. *The Closing of the American Mind*. New York: Simon & Schuster, 1987.

Bonhoeffer, Dietrich. *Creation and Fall*. New York: Collier Books, 1959.

Boorstin, Daniel. *The Genius of American Politics*. Chicago: University of Chicago Press, 1953.

Boyer, Ernest, and Fred Hechinger. *Higher Learning in the Nation's Service*. Washington, DC: Carnegie Foundation for the Advancement of Teaching, 1981.

Buckley, William F., Jr. *Gratitude: Reflections on What We Owe to Our Country*. New York: Random House, 1990.

Carnegie Council on Policy Studies in Higher Education. *Giving Youth a Better Chance: Options for Education, Work and Service*. San Francisco: Jossey-Bass, 1979.

Carnegie Foundation for the Advancement of Teaching. *A Nation at Risk: The Imperative of Educational Reform*. Washington, DC: Carnegie Foundation, 1983.

Carter, L. Stephen. *Reflections of an Affirmative Action Baby.* New York: Basic Books, 1991.

Chesterton, G. K. *What I Saw in America.* New York: De Capo Press, 1968.

Daly, Herman E., and Cobb, John B. *For the Common Good.* Boston: Beacon Press, 1989.

de Tocqueville, Alexis. *The Ancient Regime and the French Revolution.* Reprint, New York: Doubleday/Anchor, 1955.

Dewey, John. *Democracy and Education.* New York: Macmillan, 1916.

Dionne, E. J. *Why Americans Hate Politics.* New York: Simon & Schuster, 1991.

D'souza, Dinesh. *Liberal Education.* New York: Free Press, 1991.

Edsall, Thomas Byrne, and Mary D. Edsall. *Chain Reaction.* New York: Norton, 1991.

Ellul, Jacques. *False Presence of the Kingdom.* New York: Seabury Press, 1972.

_____. *The New Demons.* New York: Seabury Press, 1973.

Elshtain, Jean Bethke. *Democracy on Trial.* New York: Basic Books, 1995.

Elshtain, Jean Bethke; William Galston; Enola Aird; and Amitai Etzioni. "A Communitarian Position on the Family." *National Civic Review* (Winter 1993): 25–35.

Ericson, Edward E. *Solzhenitsyn: The Moral Vision.* Grand Rapids: Eerdmans, 1980.

Felder, Cain Hope. *Troubling Biblical Waters.* Maryknoll, NY: Orbis Books, 1989.

Glendon, Mary Ann. *Rights Talk.* New York: Free Press, 1992.

Gordon, Wayne. *Real Hope in Chicago.* Grand Rapids: Zondervan, 1995.

Guinness, Os. *The American Hour.* New York: Free Press, 1993.

Habermas, Jurgen. *Knowledge and Interests.* Boston: Beacon Press, 1971.

Havel, Václav. *Living in Truth.* Edited by Jan Vadislav. London: Faber & Faber, 1987.

_____. *Disturbing the Peace.* Translated by Paul Wilson. New York Vintage Books, 1991 .

Heimert, Alan. *Religion and the American Mind.* Cambridge: Harvard University Press, 1966.

Hofstadter, Richard. *Anti-Intellectualism in American Life.* New York: Knopf, 1963.

Horne, Gerald, ed. *Thinking and Rethinking U.S. History*. New York: Council on Interracial Books for Children, 1988.

Hughes, Robert. "Pulling the Fuse on Culture." *Time* (August 7, 1995).

Hull, Gretchen Gaebelein. *Equal to Serve*. Old Tappan, NJ: Fleming H. Revell, 1987.

Hunter, James Davison, and Os Guinness, eds. *Articles of Faith, Articles of Peace*. Washington, DC: Brookings Institution, 1990.

Kammen, Michael. *People of Paradox: An Inquiry Concerning the Origins of American Civilization*. New York: Knopf, 1972.

Kozol, Jonathan. *Savage Inequalities*. New York: Crown, 1991.

Kolakowski, Leszek. "The Idolatry of Politics." In *Modernity on Endless Trial*. Translated by Stefan Czerniawski et al. Chicago: University of Chicago Press, 1990.

Larsen, Dale, and Sandy Larsen. *While Creation Waits*. Wheaton, IL: Harold Shaw, 1992.

Lasch, Christopher. *The True and Only Heaven*. New York: Norton, 1991.

Levine, Arthur. *When Dreams and Heroes Died*. San Francisco: Jossey-Bass, 1981.

Limbaugh, Rush. *The Way Things Ought to Be*. New York: Pocket Books, 1992.

Lippmann, Walter. *The Public Philosophy*. New York: New American Library, 1955

MacIntyre, Alasdair. *After Virtue*. Notre Dame, IN: University of Notre Dame Press, 1981.

Madison, James. *Letters and Other Writings*. Philadelphia: Lippincott, 1867.

Matthews, Merrill, Jr. "Let Charities Do Welfare." *Christianity Today* (April 24, 1995).

May, F. Henry. *Ideas, Faiths and Feelings*. Oxford: Oxford University Press, 1983).

Mead, Loren. *The Once and Future Church*. New York: Alban Institute, 1991.

Medved, Michael. *Hollywood vs. America*. New York: HarperCollins, 1992.

Murray, John Courtney. *We Hold These Truths: Catholic Reflections on the American Proposition*. New York: Sheed & Ward, 1960.

Miller, Perry. *Nature's Nation*. Cambridge: Harvard University Press, 1967.

Miller, Lee William. *The First Liberty*. New York: Knopf, 1986.

Moskos, Charles C. *A Call to Civic Service: National Service for Country and Community.* New York: Free Press, 1988.

Mouw, Richard J. *Uncommon Decency: Christian Civility in an Uncivil World.* Downers Grove: InterVarsity Press, 1991.

Murray, John Courtney. *We Hold These Truths.* New York: Sheed & Ward, 1960.

Neuhaus, Richard J. *The Naked Public Square: Religion and Democracy in America.* Grand Rapids: Eerdmans, 1986.

Niebuhr, Reinhold. *The Children of Light and the Children of Darkness.* New York: Scribner's, 1947.

____. *The Irony of American History.* New York: Scribner's, 1952.

Noll, Mark. *The Scandal of the Evangelical Mind.* Grand Rapids: Eerdmans, 1994.

Oakeshott, Michael. *The Voice of Liberal Learning.* New Haven: Yale University Press, 1989.

Offner, Paul. "Welfare Didn't Do It." *Washington Post Weekly Edition* (March 20–26, 1995).

Olasky, Marvin. *The Tragedy of American Compassion.* Washington, DC: Regnery Gateway, 1992.

Padover, Saul K., ed. *The Complete Madison.* Reprint, Milwood, NY: Kraus, 1953.

Pfeffer, Leo. *Creeds in Competition.* New York: Harper & Brothers, 1958.

Phillips, Kevin P. *Post-Conservative America.* New York: Vintage Books, 1983.

Piven, Frances Fox, and Richard H. Cloward. *Why Americans Don't Vote.* New York: Pantheon, 1988.

Previte, Mary Taylor. *Hungry Ghosts.* Grand Rapids: Zondervan, 1994.

Ravitch, Diane, and Chester E. Finn, Jr. *What Do Our Seventeen-Year-Olds Know? The First National Assessment of What American Students Know About History and Literature.* New York: Harper & Row, 1987.

Reed, Ralph. *Politically Incorrect.* Dallas: Word Books, 1994.

Reichley, A. James. *Religion in American Public Life.* Washington, DC: Brookings Institution, 1985.

Rodriguez, Richard. *Hunger of Memory: The Education of Richard Rodriguez.* Boston: David R. Godine, 1981.

Rosado, Caleb. "America the Brutal." *Christianity Today* (August 15, 1994).

Rossiter, Clinton. *The Political Thought of the American Revolution.* New York: Harvest Books, 1963.

Rushdoony, Rousas J. *The Biblical Philosophy of History.* Nutley, NJ: Craig Press, 1969.

Schlesinger, Arthur, Jr. *The Disuniting of America: Reflections on a Multicultural Society.* New York: Whittle Communications, 1991.

Schmidt, Thomas J. *Straight and Narrow: Compassion and Clarity in the Homosexuality Debate.* Downers Grove, IL: InterVarsity Press, 1995.

Shklar, Judith N. *American Citizenship: The Quest for Inclusion.* Cambridge: Harvard University Press, 1991.

Sine, Tom. *Cease Fire: Searching for Sanity in America's Culture Wars.* Grand Rapids: Eerdmans, 1995.

Skillen, James W. *Christian Principle or Civil Religion: What Drives the 'Contract with the American Family'?* Washington, DC: Center for Public Justice.

Strauss, Leo. *Natural Right and History.* Ithaca, NY: Cornell University Press, 1953.

Surratt, Marshall N. "Can Media 'Get' Religion?" *Christianity Today* (July 19, 1993).

Taylor, Charles. *The Malaise of Modernity.* Concord, Ontario: House of Anansi Press, 1991.

Tinder, Glenn. *Political Thinking.* Boston: Little, Brown, 1986.

Vile, John R. "Political Rhetoric and the Need for Integrity." *Prism* (February 1995).

Walzer, Michael. *Citizenship and Civil Society.* Rutgers, NJ: New Jersey Committee for the Humanities Series on the Culture of Community, 1992, part 1.

Warren, Robert Penn. *The Legacy of the Civil War.* Cambridge: Harvard University Press, 1983.

Weber, Max. *The Protestant Ethic and the Spirit of Capitalism.* New York: Scribner's, 1958.

Weigel, Van B. *Earth Cancer.* Westport, CT: Praeger, 1995.

Weil, Simone. *The Need for Roots.* London: Routledge & Kegan Paul, 1952.

Whitehead, Barbara Dafoe. "Dan Quayle Was Right." *Atlantic Monthly* (April 1993), 47–84.

____. "Children in Crisis." *Fortune* (August 10, 1992).

Whitehead, Barbara Dafoe, and Daniel Patrick Moynihan. "Defining Deviancy Down." *American Scholar* (Winter 1993): 17–30.

Wills, Garry. *Under God: Religion and American Politics*. New York: Simon & Schuster, 1990.

Wolfe, Alan. *Whose Keeper? Social Science and Moral Obligation*. Berkeley: University of California Press, 1989.

Wuthnow, Robert. *The Restructuring of American Religion*. Princeton, NJ: Princeton University Press, 1988.

Notes

Chapter One: Evangelical Moderates: Alone in America

1. Editorial, *The Nation* (November 28, 1994), 633.
2. Pat Buchanan in his address at the Christian Coalition's Road to Victory conference on September 9, 1995.
3. Cited by John C. Green, James L. Guth, Lyman A. Kellstedt, and Corwin E. Smidt in *Christian Century* (July 5–12, 1995), 677.
4. *Time* (November 20, 1995), 66.

Chapter Two: How "Christian" Is the Coalition?

1. Ralph Reed in his opening address at the Christian Coalition's Road to Victory conference on September 8, 1995.
2. Mike Huckabee in his address at the Christian Coalition's Road to Victory conference on September 9, 1995.
3. John R. Vile, "Political Rhetoric and the Need for Integrity," *Prism* (February 1995), 26.
4. Ibid.
5. Ralph Reed, Road to Victory conference, September 8, 1995.
6. This information is based on author Randall L. Frame's personal interview with one of the protestors.
7. As quoted by James Walsh in "Spirit of Sisterhood," *Time* (September 18, 1995), 79.
8. Mike Huckabee at the Road to Victory conference, September 9, 1995.

Chapter Three: Preserving the Church's Unique Mission

1. Dan Coats in his address at the Christian Coalition's Road to Victory conference on September 8, 1995.
2. Christopher A. Hall in an unpublished article.

Chapter Four: The Pathology of Ideology

1. From a telephone poll conducted for *Time*/CNN by Yankelovich Partners Inc., as reported in *Time* (April 10, 1995), 35.
2. James Davison Hunter, *Culture Wars* (New York: Basic Books, 1991), 156.
3. See Rush Limbaugh, *The Way Things Ought to Be* (New York: Pocket Books, 1992), 53.

Chapter Five: The Ten Commandments of Moderate Political Behavior

1. Loren Mead, *The Once and Future Church* (New York: Alban Institute, 1991), 44.

2. Mark Noll, *The Scandal of the Evangelical Mind* (Grand Rapids: Eerdmans, 1994), 125–26.

3. Robert Wuthnow in a review symposium, "The Scandal of the Evangelical Mind," *First Things* (March 1995), 41.

4. *National & International Religion Report* (November 28, 1994).

5. Gretchen Gaebelein Hull, *Equal to Serve* (Old Tappan, NJ: Revell, 1987), 59.

6. Ralph Reed, *Politically Incorrect* (Dallas: Word Books, 1994), 9.

7. Noll, *The Scandal of the Evangelical Mind,* 12.

8. Ibid., 14.

9. Ralph Reed in his opening address at the Christian Coalition's 1995 Road to Victory conference, September 8, 1995.

10. From a 1991 readership survey by *Christianity Today* as reported by Executive Editor David Neff in a 1995 speech at Eastern College in St. Davids, Pennsylvania.

11. Ray Bakke in an Open Letter on "Family Values" to Sharon Benson of Burlington, Washington, in February 1993.

12. *Christianity Today* (July 14, 1989), 42.

Chapter Six: The American Experiment

1. Rush Limbaugh, *The Way Things Ought to Be* (New York: Basic Books, 1992), 45.

2. Gerald Horne, ed., *Thinking and Rethinking U.S. History* (New York: Council on Interracial Books for Children, 1988), 6.

3. Ibid., 7.

4. Ibid., 20.

5. James W. Skillen, "Christian Principle or Civil Religion: What Drives the 'Contract with the American Family'?" (Washington, DC: Center for Public Justice, n.d.).

6. Horne, *Thinking and Rethinking U.S. History,* 21.

7. Ibid., 37.

8. *Christianity Today* (July 18, 1994), 33.

9. Dale and Sandy Larsen, *While Creation Waits* (Wheaton, IL: Harold Shaw, 1992), 47.

10. John Wesley, "Thoughts on Slavery," in Horne, *Thinking and Rethinking U.S. History,* 49.

11. Horne, *Thinking and Rethinking U.S. History,* 32.

12. Vincent Harding, *There Is a River*, as recorded in Horne, *Thinking and Rethinking U.S. History*, 48.

13. Mrs. Michelle Easton on a Focus on the Family radio program in 1996, titled "Goals 2000: History Redefined."

14. Horne, *Thinking and Rethinking U.S. History*, 39.

15. Gerald R. McDermott, "What Jonathan Edwards Can Teach Us About Politics," *Christianity Today* (July 18, 1994), 32.

Chapter Seven: Church Versus State

1. Ralph Reed, *Politically Incorrect* (Dallas: Word Books, 1994), 76.

2. James W. Skillen, "Christian Principle or Civil Religion: What Drives the 'Contract with the American Family'?" (Washington, DC: Center for Public Justice, n.d.).

3. Mark Noll, *The Scandal of the Evangelical Mind* (Grand Rapids: Eerdmans, 1994), 65.

4. Ibid.

5. Ibid., 64.

6. John R. Vile, "Political Rhetoric and the Need for Integrity," *Prism* (February 1995), 26.

7. Steve McFarland in the speech "Free Religious Expression in a 'Politically Correct' World," at a Church and State Conference at Westminster Theological Seminary in Philadelphia in 1992.

8. *Christianity Today* (November 14, 1994), 74.

9. *Christianity Today* (August 14, 1995), 57.

10. *Christianity Today* (April 14, 1995), 18.

11. Reed, *Politically Incorrect*, 44.

12. Tom Sine, *Cease Fire: Searching for Sanity in America's Culture Wars* (Grand Rapids: Eerdmans, 1995), 238.

Chapter Eight: The Role of Government

1. Joe Morse, *Time* (May 22, 1995), 14.

2. Charles Stenholm in his address at the Christian Coalition's Road to Victory conference on September 8, 1995.

3. The document, available from the Center for Public Justice, is called "A New Vision for Welfare Reform." A larger treatment of this issue is contained in *Welfare in America: Christian Perspectives on a Policy in Crisis* (Grand Rapids: Eerdmans, 1995).

4. Dick Armey in his address at the Christian Coalition's Road to Victory conference on September 8, 1995.

5. Ralph Reed in his address at the Christian Coalition's Road to Victory conference on September 9, 1995.

6. William Bennett in his address at the Christian Coalition's Road to Victory conference on September 8, 1995.

7. James W. Skillen, "Christian Principle or Civil Religion: What Drives the 'Contract with the American Family'?" (Washington, DC: Center for Public Justice, n.d.).

8. Tom Sine, *Cease Fire: Searching for Sanity in America's Culture Wars* (Grand Rapids: Eerdmans, 1995), 132.

9. *Business Week* (April 25, 1994)..

10. James K. Glassman, "An Automatic Conclusion," *Washington Post* (February 13–19, 1995), 36.

11. Ralph Reed, *Politically Incorrect* (Dallas: Word, 1994), 33.

Chapter Nine: Welfare

1. Marvin Olasky, *The Tragedy of American Compassion* (Washington, DC: Regnery Gateway, 1992), 42.

2. Merrill Matthews, Jr., "Let Charities Do Welfare," *Christianity Today* (April 24, 1995), 7.

3. Paul Offner, "Welfare Didn't Do It," *Washington Post Weekly Edition* (March 20–26, 1995), 29.

4. Ray Bakke in an Open Letter on "Family Values" to Sharon Benson of Burlington, Washington, in February 1993.

5. Gilbert M. Gaul and Susan Q. Stranahan, "A Successful Program, or Millions Down the Drain?" *Philadelphia Inquirer* (June 9, 1995), 1.

6. Ibid., "How billions in taxes failed to create jobs," *Philadelphia Inquirer* (June 4, 1995), 1.

7. Ibid.

8. Dana Priest, "Billions Gone AWOL," *Washington Post Weekly Edition* (May 22–28, 1995), 6.

9. Karen Tumulty, "Budget, Meet Thy Maker," *Time* (February 27, 1995), 19.

10. Ralph Reed, *Politically Incorrect* (Dallas: Word, 1994), 10.

11. Ibid., 35.

12. Laurie Goodstein, "Can Churches Be Everyone's Keeper?" *Washington Post Weekly Edition* (March 6–12, 1995), 31.

13. Ibid.

14. Mike Huckabee in his address at the Christian Coalition's Road to Victory conference on September 9, 1995.

15. *Christianity Today* (April 24, 1995), 48.

16. "A Less Patronizing Welfare Debate," *Washington Post Weekly Edition* (July 3–9, 1995), 27.

17. Barbara Vobejda, "Welfare Check, Reality Check," *Washington Post Weekly Edition* (March 13–19, 1995), 7.

18. Ibid.

Chapter Ten: Abortion

1. William F. Buckley, "Listening to Mr. Right," *Christianity Today* (October 2, 1995), 36.

2. Charles Colson, "Pro-Life Powder Keg," *Christianity Today* (April 24, 1995), 64.

3. Jill Smolowe, "Fear in the Land," *Time* (January 16, 1995), 34.

4. "Clinic Killings Motivate Push to Silence Pro-Life Protest," *Christianity Today* (March 6, 1995).

5. Gretchen Gaebelein Hull, *Equal to Serve* (Old Tappan, NJ: Revell, 1987), 42.

6. Keynote address at the Third International Conference of Christians for Biblical Equality, Wheaton College, 1993.

7. Robert Casey in his address at the Christian Coalition's 1995 Road to Victory conference on September 8, 1995.

Chapter Eleven: "Family Values"

1. *New Republic* 207, no. 16 (October 12, 1992): 34.
2. Thomas J. Schmidt, *Straight and Narrow: Compassion and Clarity in the Homosexuality Debate* (Downers Grove, IL: InterVarsity, 1995).
3. Douglas J. Besharov, "Sinking Family Values," a book review article in the *Washington Post Weekly Edition* (January 30–Feburary 5, 1995), 36.
4. *National & International Religion Report* (April 17, 1995).
5. Besharov, "Sinking Family Values," 36.
6. Barbara Vobejda, "Daddy's Home, But Not With His Kids," *Washington Post Weekly Edition* (May 1–7, 1995), 34.
7. Ibid.
8. Murray Dubin, "More Grandparents Are Doing the Parenting," *Philadelphia Inquirer* (May 3, 1995), H1.
9. Barbara Dafoe Whitehead, interviewed by Peggy Noonan for a segment of the public television series *On Values* that was broadcast in 1995.
10. Ibid.
11. Ibid.
12. Robert Casey in his address at the Christian Coalition's Road to Victory conference on September 8, 1995.
13. This is quoted from a paper that Van Leeuwen wrote in conjunction with a program of the Center for Public Justice.
14. Cain Hope Felder, *Troubling Biblical Waters* (Maryknoll, NY: Orbis, 1989), 156.
15. Ibid., 151.
16. Tom Sine, *Cease Fire: Searching for Sanity in America's Culture Wars* (Grand Rapids: Eerdmans, 1995), 142.
17. Mrs. Linda Page on a Focus on the Family radio program in 1995 titled "Goals 2000: History Redefined."
18. Loren Mead, *The Once and Future Church* (New York: Alban Institute, 1991), 2.
19. Stanley Crouch was interviewed by Peggy Noonan for a segment of the public television series *On Values* that was broadcast in 1995.
20. Caleb Rosado, "America the Brutal," *Christianity Today* (August 15, 1994), 20.
21. Ralph Reed, *Politically Incorrect* (Dallas: Word Books, 1994), 36.
22. Besharov, "Sinking Family Values," 36.

Chapter Twelve: The Justice System

1. Charles Colson in a *Breakpoint* radio commentary series on crime.
2. Pierre Thomas, "Our 'Subculture of Violence,'" *Washington Post Weekly Edition* (March 20–26, 1995), 37.
3. *USA Today* (December 1–3, 1995), 1A.
4. Randy Frame, "A Matter of Life and Death," *Christianity Today* (August 14, 1995), 50.
5. Thomas E. Schmidt, *Straight & Narrow: Compassion and Clarity in the Homosexuality Debate* (Downers Grove, IL: InterVarsity, 1995), 131.

6. John J. Dilulio, Jr., "True Welfare Reform," *Washington Post Weekly Edition* (January 23–29, 1995).

7. Ibid.

8. Mary Taylor Previte, *Hungry Ghosts* (Grand Rapids: Zondervan, 1994), 72.

9. Dilulio, "True Welfare Reform."

10. Previte, *Hungry Ghosts,* 172, 254.

11. Ibid., 129.

12. Ibid., 175.

13. Ibid., 252.

14. Wayne Gordon, *Real Hope in Chicago* (Grand Rapids: Zondervan, 1995), 137.

15. Previte, *Hungry Ghosts,* 97.

16. Ibid., 251.

17. Ibid., 123.

18. Caleb Rosado, "America the Brutal," *Christianity Today* (Aguust 15, 1994), 20.

19. Moody Action insert (sic) in the July–August 1995 issue of *Moody Monthly* magazine.

Chapter Thirteen: Homosexuality, Racism, the Media, the Environment, and Foreign Policy

1. William F. Buckley in an interview in "Listening to Mr. Right," *Christianity Today* (October 2, 1995), 36.

2. John Huffman, Jr., in an interview in "Sex Wars Strategist," *Christianity Today* (November 22, 1993), 10.

3. Edward G. Dobson, "A Journey of Love," *Prism* (May–June 1995), 11.

4. Thomas E. Schmidt, *Straight and Narrow: Compassion and Clarity in the Homosexuality Debate* (Downers Grove, IL: InterVarsity, 1995), 162.

5. Ibid., 161–62.

6. "Report: Federal Spending on AIDS Tops Cancer, Heart Disease—Despite Far Fewer Deaths," *Lambda Report* (February–March, 1995), 1.

7. Michael Medved, *Hollywood vs. America* (New York: HarperCollins, 1992), 312.

8. Huffman, "Sex Wars Strategist," 10.

9. Schmidt, *Straight and Narrow,* 11.

10. Greg Louganis with Eric Marcus in "Louganis' Childhood and Early Gay Feelings," *Philadelphia Inquirer* (March 13, 1995), G8.

11. Ray Bakke in an Open Letter on "Family Values" to Sharon Benson of Burlington, Washington, in February 1993.

12. Ralph Reed, *Politically Incorrect* (Dallas: Word, 1994), 5.

13. See Caleb Rosado, "America the Brutal," *Christianity Today* (August 15, 1994), 20.

14. Cain Hope Felder, *Troubling Biblical Waters* (Maryknoll, NY: Orbis, 1989), 8.

15. Ibid., 22.

16. Jeremiah A. Wright, Jr., "Afrocentricity and the Christian Faith," a lecture given at Eastern Baptist Theological Seminary in Philadelphia on February 21, 1995.

17. Carl F. Ellis, "Afrocentrism and Christianity: Complement or Conflict?" *Urban Family* (Summer 1995), 15.

18. Ibid.

19. Stanley Crouch was interviewed by Peggy Noon for a segment of the public television series *On Values* that was broadcast during 1995.

20. Ibid.

21. Jonathan Storm, "Off-color Television: Prime-time Shows Dirtying Up Their Act," *Philadelphia Inquirer* (November 26, 1995), 1.

22. Howard Kurtz, "A Great Divide Between the Media and the Public," *Washington Post National Weekly Edition* (May 29–June 4, 1995), 7.

23. Ibid.

24. Marshall N. Surratt, "Can Media 'Get' Religion?" *Christianity Today* (July 19, 1993), 15.

25. The survey, called "Bridging the Gap: Religion and the News Media," was conducted by John Dart and Jimmy Allen.

26. *National & International Religion Report* (April 17, 1995), 6.

27. Storm, "Off-color Television," 1.

28. Medved, *Hollywood vs. America*, 112.

29. Barbara Dafoe Whitehead was interviewed by Peggy Noonan for a segment of the public television series *On Values* that was broadcast in 1995.

30. Medved, *Hollywood vs. America*, 312.

31. Ibid., 313.

32. *Christianity Today* (September 11, 1995), 58.

33. Robert Hughes, "Pulling the Fuse on Culture," *Time* (August 7, 1995), 61.

34. Ibid.

35. Francis Schaeffer, *Pollution and the Death of Man: The Christian View of Ecology* (Wheaton, IL: Tyndale House, 1970), 70.

36. Genesis 1:29 states that God gave the human beings he created "every seed-bearing plant and every tree that has fruit with seed in it" to be used for food.

37. Herman E. Daly and John B. Cobb, Jr., *For the Common Good* (Boston: Beacon Press, 1989), 104.

38. Ibid.

39. Ibid.

40. Karl Barth, *The Doctrine of Creation,* vol. III, part 4 in *Church Dogmatics* (Edinburgh: T. & T. Clark, 1961), 354.

41. Rush Limbaugh, *The Way Things Ought to Be* (New York: Basic Books, 1992), 160.

42. Mark Jaffe, "In Global Warming, It's a Question of Degree," *Philadelphia Inquirer* (October 25, 1995), 1.

43. Personal interview.

44. Unpublished article.

45. Ibid.

46. Tom Kenworthy, "Letting the Truth Fall Where It May," *Washington Post National Weekly Edition* (March 27–April 2, 1995), 31.

47. Fen Montaigne, "Will Congress Put Nation's Environmental Gains at Risk?" *Philadelphia Inquirer* (July 16, 1995), C1.

48. Randy Frame, "Quick Change Artists," *Christianity Today* (December 12, 1994), 50.

49. "Should America Stay the Course in Somalia?" *Christianity Today* (November 22, 1993), 48.

50. Ibid.

51. Richard Morin, "Foreign Aid: Mired in Misunderstanding," *Washington Post Weekly Edition* (March 20–26, 1995), 37.

52. *Christianity Today* (April 24, 1995), 50.

Chapter Fourteen: A Political Agenda for Evangelical Moderates

1. Ralph Reed, *Politically Incorrect* (Dallas: Word Books, 1994), 27.

2. Robert A. Eberle, *Time* (June 5, 1995), 6.

3. Tom Price, "The Mounting Stakes of Our Casino Economy," *Christianity Today* (April 8, 1996), 98.

4. See *Prism* (July–August 1995), 2.

5. Ibid.